Meeting the Needs of Students with Dyslexia

Also available from Network Continuum:
Inclusion in Schools: Making a Difference – Rosemary Sage

Available from Continuum:
100 Ideas for Supporting Pupils with Dyslexia – Gavin Reid and Shannon Green
Dyslexia (2nd edition) – Gavin Reid
The Teaching Assistant's Guide to Dyslexia – Gavin Reid and Shannon Green
SENCO At A Glance: A Toolkit for Success – Linda Evans

Meeting the Needs of Students with Dyslexia

June Massey

network
continuum

Continuum International Publishing Group
Network Continuum
The Tower Building   80 Maiden Lane, Suite 704
11 York Road   New York, NY 10038
SE1 7NX

www.networkcontinuum.co.uk
www.continuumbooks.com

British Library Cataloguing-in-Publication Data
A catalogue record for this book is available from the British Library.

ISBN: 9781855394452 (paperback)

Library of Congress Cataloguing-in-Publication Data
A catalog record for this book is available from the Library of Congress.

Typeset by YHT Ltd, London
Printed and bound in Great Britain by Cromwell Press, Wiltshire

Contents

Acknowledgements

This book is dedicated to Ron Radley, Anne Harris and my family.

With thanks to Joan Ashley, Simon and Ruth Bendall, Mary Holland, Michael Massey, Robin Tod and Emily Stowe for their comments and assistance, Steve Chinn for allowing me to use his ideas about 'inchworms and grasshoppers', and to the British Dyslexia Association for allowing me to use their definition of dyslexia as a starting point. Thanks also to Bridget Gibbs and Alison Clark at Network Continuum for making the whole process as painless as possible.

My greatest debt of gratitude is owed to all my students and colleagues, past and present, from whom I have learned so much.

Introduction

There is now, thankfully, a greater awareness of dyslexia and the lifelong implications for learning, socio-emotional issues and employment. My experience has shown that, during statutory education, recognition of signs of dyslexia, ongoing assessment and targeted teaching, both as structured individual programmes and within the classroom, have proved extremely beneficial in terms of achievement and self-esteem which continues throughout the student's life.

My experience has also shown that, although there are many excellent, concise definitions of dyslexia, the range of difficulties, differences and degree of impact of dyslexia on an individual's learning and everyday life means that each will have a unique 'definition' that is specific to him or her. Discovering the individual student's strengths, weaknesses and different ways of thinking and helping him or her to capitalize on them has made my work as a specialist teacher and assessor incredibly rewarding.

Literacy and numeracy skills, at all stages of lifelong learning, are given equal importance. As one who teaches numeracy, I am aware that many teachers and support staff feel that they do not have sufficient working knowledge of the impact of dyslexia on numeracy and maths. Consequently, I felt it important that a significant part of this book should be devoted to this topic.

The book is structured to enable teachers and support staff to relate strategies for the management of dyslexia to both the underlying theories about dyslexia and the first-hand experiences of students and practitioners in their day-to-day lives.

I have designed this book to be a guide which busy teachers and support staff can 'dip in to' as the need arises. It is a mistake to think that there are 'hard and fast rules' to adhere to when working with dyslexic students; each will have their own different ways of learning and will need to be supported to develop different strategies to accommodate these. When considering strategies to help the dyslexic student, each teacher will need to consider not only the individual student's needs, but the learning needs of other students, the subject matter to be taught, available resources and the teacher's own preferred teaching style.

Many teachers are pleasantly surprised to realize that they already incorporate many strategies within their classrooms and that it would need very little work to accommodate others in their teaching. For those who wish, or need, to investigate some aspects of dyslexia or teaching in greater depth, I have made suggestions for further reading throughout the book. A list of useful contacts, further reading and list of suppliers of specialist materials and publications can be found at the end.

Although this book is primarily aimed at those involved in the learning experience of students in primary and secondary schools, the difficulties encountered and strategies suggested could be relevant to educationalists working in the post-compulsory sector.

I hope that this book can be used to help to enhance the learning experience of the dyslexic students and the teaching experience of all those involved in the student's learning.

The student (apart from in case studies) is referred to as masculine and teachers and others referred to as feminine. This is purely to help with ease of reading and is not intended to be make assumptions or be discriminatory.

Dyslexia: Definition, recognition and assessment

1

Definition

For every ten books on dyslexia there are likely to be 11 definitions. The British Dyslexia Association has kindly given permission to quote their version which covers the key characteristics of dyslexia.

> Dyslexia is a specific learning difficulty which is neurobiological in origin and persists across the lifespan.
>
> It is characterised by difficulties with phonological processing, rapid naming, working memory, processing speed and the automatic development of skills that are unexpected in relation to an individual's other cognitive abilities.
>
> These processing difficulties can undermine the acquisition of literacy and numeracy skills, as well as musical notation, and have an effect on verbal communication, organisation and adaptation to change.
>
> Their impact can be mitigated by correct teaching, strategy development and the use of information technology. (British Dyslexia Association 2007)

Facts

- The word 'dyslexia' derives from the Greek words '*dys*' (difficult) and '*lexis*' (words) and literally means 'difficulty with words'.
- About 10 per cent of the population is affected by dyslexia to varying degrees.
- Recent research, including that of Fisher et al. (1999), indicates a likely genetic predisposition to dyslexia in a significant proportion of dyslexic individuals.
- Dyslexia occurs across the range of intellectual ability.
- It is found in all racial, linguistic and socio-economic backgrounds.
- Dyslexia will occur within a normal teaching environment.

- Some dyslexic individuals will use sound problem-solving skills to develop effective strategies for accommodating dyslexia.
- Signs of dyslexia can often be found in other specific learning difficulties.
- The degree of impact and nature of difficulties will vary from person to person.
- Dyslexia is one of many factors that may cause difficulties with reading and spelling. Extended or chronic illness, poor school attendance, changing schools, teaching, socio-emotional problems and other specific learning difficulties can affect the acquisition of literacy skills.
- The impact of dyslexia on learning may become increasingly obvious as the expectation of skills levels increases.
- Dyslexia need not be a barrier to success. Dyslexic individuals have found success in the fields of sport, music, art, the acting profession, business and academia (Einstein was, allegedly, dyslexic).
- 'Some learners have very well developed creative skills and/or interpersonal skills, others have strong oral skills. Some have no outstanding talents. All have strengths' (British Dyslexia Association 2006).

> **'All have strengths' is a crucial phrase to keep in mind. Meeting the learning, social and emotional needs of the dyslexic student requires the recognition, appreciation and use of his strengths in addition to accommodating his weaknesses.**

Neurology

The brain is divided into two hemispheres, the left and right hemispheres. Figure 1 shows the characteristics of the right and left brain. Briefly, the left brain will process information sequentially, focusing on smaller tasks and the right will take a holistic 'whole picture' approach. The left brain handles processing that involves language, including phonological processing, and sequential processing. The right brain will process visual and spatial information which can include music. There are theories that the right brain also takes a larger share of the control of emotion.

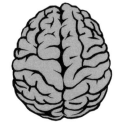

LEFT (sequential, linear)

- Logical
- Orderly, likes lists
- Systematic, sequential
- Prefers detailed processing/sees small details
- Deals with one thing at a time
- Prefers writing things down
- Works 'consciously'
- Uses language definition to describe
- Analyses
- Mechanical
- Thinks in words and symbols
- Prefers to find cause and effect

RIGHT (Holistic, global)

- Creative
- Intuitive
- Imaginative
- Finds immediate 'solutions'
- Quickly gets an overview of a problem
- Can multitask
- Sees the whole picture (Gestalt)
- Works 'subconsciously'
- Uses images, shapes and colour to describe
- Synthesises
- Musical, artistic
- Thinks in pictures and designs
- Looks for inter-relationships

Figure 1 Left and right brain functions

Theories that the structure of the dyslexic brain differed from that of the non-dyslexic were substantiated by the work of Geschwind and Levitsky (1968) and Galaburda et al. (1987). During autopsy, the two hemispheres of the brains of dyslexic individuals were found to be symmetrical whereas the left hemispheres of non-dyslexic individuals were, on the whole, found to be larger. Rapid advancement of technology has now meant that Functional Imaging can now be used to record the activity occurring in different areas of the brain while the individual is performing an information processing task such as reading, listening to instructions, writing, or mathematical computations. Paulascu, Frith and Snowling (1995) published the PET scan study results which showed that there was less activity in the left hemisphere of the dyslexic brain when the individual was performing a phonological processing task. Further complex neurological study has been carried out which has led to the conclusion by experts in the field that there is consistent evidence of differences between dyslexic and other brains.

It is common to find that the right-brained dyslexic student is artistic, a creative thinker and possesses excellent problem-solving skills, although it is wrong to assume that all dyslexic students will automatically take interest in, or find success in archetypal 'right-brained' activities.

Those teachers who are aware of the characteristics of right- and left-brained processing may have self-assessed their own dominance. Some of my colleagues have taken a hemispheric dominance test and been quite surprised by a result that does not match their self-perception. There are several tests available on the internet (use a search engine such as Google and type in 'hemispheric dominance inventory test'). It is a valuable exercise to reflect on whether your dominant style influences your teaching style.

Dyslexia as a specific learning difficulty/difference

The term 'specific learning difficulty' encompasses a broad spectrum of signs that are often categorized under 'labels'. Thus, a student who exhibits signs that are largely found under the 'dyslexia' heading may be said to 'exhibit a profile that is consistent with dyslexia'. A similar statement may occur for students who exhibit traits of, for example, dyspraxia, Asperger's syndrome, Attention Deficit Disorder (ADD), Attention Deficit Hyperactivity Disorder (ADHD) or dyscalculia.

Some practitioners prefer to use the term 'specific learning difference' rather than 'difficulty' to highlight the fact that dyslexic students think and learn differently. In fact, one of the greatest pleasures I have found in working with dyslexic students is derived from gaining an insight into different ways of learning, often discovering new and innovative ways of tackling problems in the process. Pollock and

Waller (1999) suggest that dyslexia should be viewed as a different learning ability that becomes a difficulty if it remains unrecognized or if inappropriate teaching results in failure to gain competency in literacy. I have tried to instil a positive approach to thinking differently in my students and most are only too willing to develop and exhibit their individuality. However, I have, on many occasions, received a response that the word 'difference' does not fully reflect the hard work that some students have to put in to accommodate their difficulties. Each teacher will doubtless have her own preference but I wish to respect the opinions of those students who feel that their 'difficulty' should be recognized.

Signs of dyslexia may also appear in 'checklists' of signs in other specific learning difficulties. For example, the dyspraxic individual is likely to have poor motor skills but the dyslexic student may also experience difficulties in this area.

There can be co-morbidity; that is, an individual may be assessed as both dyslexia and dyspraxic or have dyspraxia and ADHD.

A diagnosis of a specific learning difficulty is not an exact science. If a person is continually sneezing and coughing and has a temperature, it can be fairly certain that he has a cold. However, if a student does not appear to be listening in class and cannot demonstrate that he has remembered or understood what the teacher has said, does the teacher know if he has ADHD, dyslexia or if he is preoccupied with social or emotional problems outside of school? The following two sections examine the signs of dyslexia and the processes required to gain a diagnosis of dyslexia.

Recognizing signs of dyslexia

The dyslexic student may exhibit any or several of the signs of dyslexia at any time in his educational career. It must also be remembered that some dyslexic students devise extraordinary compensatory strategies that eventually become less effective as the increasing amount and complexity of information encountered place a greater strain on weak memory or processing skills. The degree of impact can vary enormously and will be influenced by the severity and areas of weakness. One student may be unable accurately to spell his own name throughout his life and another may not experience problems until he needs to revise extensively or write higher-level essays.

The following lists are not checklists as the student may only 'tick a few boxes', creating a dilemma for the teacher who may ask 'how many ticks constitute a concern?' Another student may not have a history which suggests the presence of dyslexia, making the teacher reluctant to express her concerns. Remember that it is never 'too late' to consider the possibility of dyslexia.

The lists, therefore, are signs that dyslexic students commonly exhibit and are intended as a guide for observation. Due to the overlap with other conditions, some may not be exclusive to dyslexia. I have tried to list as many general signs as possible without making this an unusable document. Do not dismiss any areas for concern because they are not listed in this or another book or website.

The signs given in this chapter are divided into the age groups in which they are most likely to appear first.

Signs of dyslexia in relationship to numeracy and maths will be found in Chapter 6.

Background information

If it is deemed necessary to assess the student for dyslexia, background information from parents is invaluable to the assessor. It will also give the teacher an insight into learning, social or emotional issues that may not be apparent in the classroom.

- Family history of dyslexia. Family members may not have had a formal diagnosis so the answer may be 'no'. If there seems to be a degree of hesitancy, ask if any family member has had difficulty with reading, spelling or writing and the answer may be 'yes'.
- History of other health problems that may have impacted on learning (including glue ear).
- Signs of lack of self-esteem/confidence.
- Signs of a reluctance to come to school/loss of interest in school work.
- Has 'good' and 'bad' days.
- Frustrated by 'clumsiness' or 'forgetfulness'.
- Ask the parents if there are other concerns or if they have noted unusual behaviours/milestones not met/unexpected difficulties.

Pre-school

- Has difficulty in recognizing rhyme (man, ran and can). Cannot remember nursery rhymes.
- Late speaker or speech was not clear.
- Mixes syllables in words (patercillar for caterpillar). All children do this to some extent but notice should be taken of the child who does this frequently or if this persists.
- Gets frustrated at inability to 'find' words he wishes to use.
- Needs repetition of simple instructions: 'get your book so that we can read it'. May appear to not be paying attention. Does not appear to be 'listening'.
- Cannot follow dialogue on childrens' television, DVD or story tape. Is likely to lose interest quickly.
- Difficulty keeping rhythm during clapping and dancing games. May not be able to match actions and words during games like 'The wheels on the bus'.
- Cannot remember the sequence of action games.
- Enjoys the experience of sharing an early book with a parent but shows no sign of matching words to pictures.

- Difficulties with gross motor skills: catching, throwing and kicking balls, regularly bumping into things or people, dropping things.
- Difficulty with fine motor skills. May get frustrated by inability to join pieces of puzzles, cannot develop an efficient grip or control when using crayons.
- Late in dressing independently.
- May not have crawled as a baby.

Key Stages 1 and 2

- Slowness in getting dressed for PE or getting coat and shoes on at playtime. May have difficulty with buttons. Looks 'untidy' when finally dressed.
- Cannot tie shoelaces. If the student can easily get dressed, this may be due to the inability to remember the processes needed rather than a difficulty with motor skills.
- Difficulty in art or practical tasks such as model-making.
- Cannot easily trace, track through mazes or keep in lines when colouring.
- Difficulty with sequencing the days of the week, months of the year and the alphabet.
- Cannot keep his drawer tidy. Is disorganized when helping to tidy up in class.
- Cannot remember longer instructions. 'Go to the cupboard and get the red exercise books' requires him to remember five separate pieces of information and instructions.
- Difficulty with remembering facts, names and dates.
- Cannot follow instructions.
- Still has difficulty with action games.
- Poor concentration when reading, writing or listening.
- May easily become 'bored' in class and could become disruptive or 'switch off'.
- Continues to get stuck when trying to 'find' words when speaking. Ask those on playground duty (see Chapter 7) to check if this impacts socially.
- Confuses left/right, up/down, forward/back.
- A discrepancy between his verbal and written ability may begin to show. Self-esteem and self-confidence may be affected.
- May start to develop avoidance tactics during reading and writing exercises in class. He may attempt to extend the plenary or discussion session, 'lose' books, drop pens or develop a host of quite imaginative tactics. This could also manifest as disruptive behaviour.
- Difficulty understanding time and tense.
- Can't match concepts with words; confuses 'noun' and 'adjective'.
- Cannot 'multitask' or remember information if doing something else at the time.
- Visual perceptual difficulties – disturbance, distortion or discomfort may be noticed (see Meares-Irlen Syndrome in Chapter 3).

Reading

- Cannot match letters and sounds. Decoding skills are weak.
- Cannot recognize syllables. Cannot segment when reading.
- Has problems with comprehension.
- Reads a word then cannot read it later in the same piece of text. May be able to do this but cannot recognize the word the following day.

- Reads slowly. Reading may not be fluent.
- Difficulty in reading aloud; mispronounces familiar words, reading is not fluent or lacks intonation, changes tenses, adds words; reads fluently but can't answer questions about what he has read.
- Cannot remember what he has read.
- Misreads words as similar-looking ones or makes semantic errors (reads 'horse' for 'pony').
- The student with a good vocabulary may hide difficulties by using contextual clues when reading silently or to himself. If this is suspected, ask the student to read to you (not in front of the class).
- Loses his place when reading or reads the same sentence twice.
- Confuses 'small' words – may read 'and' as 'but'.
- Lack of interest in reading for pleasure.
- May read the bare minimum necessary to gain information.
- May exhibit difficulties with motor skills during practical tasks.

Spelling and writing

- Transposition of letters within words (two and tow). This can also happen when reading.
- Reversal of letters: 'b' written as 'd'.
- Cannot remember spelling patterns and rules.
- Leaves letters or syllables out of words or adds syllables (rememember for remember).
- Gives 'bizarre' spellings that bear similarity to the word attempted ('clibsic' for bicycle).
- Cannot recognize spelling errors.
- Spells the same word in different ways on different days.
- Substitutes 'small' words for others ('a boy walked down and road' instead of 'a boy walked down the road').
- Content of written answers is not as full as verbal explanations.
- Uses more complex or imaginative vocabulary when speaking than when writing.
- Takes longer than his peers to complete written tasks.
- Poor handwriting and/or pen control.
- He may become a reluctant writer if self-perception of his written work is low, especially when there is a noticeable discrepancy between his verbal and written ability.

Key Stages 3 and 4 and adult

The word 'adult' is included as it is not uncommon for teachers and parents, in the course of investigating the impact of the student's dyslexia, to recognize similar traits in themselves.

All of the above signs may continue into secondary education and adulthood. Be aware that these may persist despite the student having received specialist help at primary school. I once heard the unhelpful comment: 'He can't be dyslexic if he's had two years of help and he still can't read.' The pace of progress in reading and writing can be very slow for some dyslexic students. Each small step should be recognized as an achievement.

During secondary education, the following may also occur:

General

- Increasing discrepancy between oral and written performance. There may be a significant difference between CAT scores and attainment scores.
- Self-esteem may continue to decrease. This is often exacerbated by the teenager's reluctance to feel 'different' from his peers. He may also not want to be seen to be doing 'easier' work.
- May become increasingly withdrawn or behaviour may become worse.
- May become increasingly de-motivated in all areas of his life.
- Organizational difficulties may result in him arriving without equipment or homework or having disorganized folders.
- He may arrive late to school or lessons or turn up at the wrong room.
- Has increasing difficulty in processing verbal information and instructions. Cannot keep up with lessons.
- Cannot take notes from speech and listen at the same time.
- Time management is poor. Leaves homework until the last minute. Cannot work out how to schedule the writing of longer assignments.
- Cannot sequence problems or follow sequences. This may show in science, maths and practical-based subjects.
- May have difficulties in some subject areas and not others. The art teacher may report that the right-brained student is her star pupil whereas the English teacher will view him as one of her struggling students.
- Finds increasing difficulty with revision.
- May have developed unusual ways of remembering things.
- May exhibit a strong preference to a style of working and learning. For example, he may record much of his work or take notes pictorially.
- Areas of strength may become more evident. He may begin to excel in art or sports. He may begin to develop innovative ways of presenting work or be an enthusiastic participant in practical work or discussion. The student should be encouraged to use his strengths for effective study.

Reading

- Difficulties with comprehension may become more pronounced.
- Previously unrecognized difficulties with reading may show as the student meets a greater amount of complex or subject-specific vocabulary. Gets lost with long words such as psychological.
- May be more likely to misread similar-looking words.
- Difficulty with skimming and scanning.

Writing and spelling

- Does not write correct or sufficient information in a homework diary to allow him to complete homework.
- Difficulty with sentence structure.
- Difficulty in planning essays.
- Cannot get thoughts onto paper. Thinks quicker than he writes.

- Copies slowly or incorrectly from the board.
- Handwriting is slow or difficult to read.
- May not check work.

The impact of dyslexia on self-esteem

The dyslexic student may spend a significant amount of his life being asked to carry out tasks that he finds difficult and he may feel that he is gaining little success. Secure learning can happen for the dyslexic student in much smaller steps than for his peers, but the hard work needed to achieve these steps must be appreciated by teachers, parents and, most importantly, the student himself. In a benchmark-driven education system it is often difficult for the dyslexic student to celebrate his achievements if he or others are constantly comparing his performance with that of his peers.

Self-esteem is lowered by poor self-perception. Dyslexic students may label themselves 'thick' or 'stupid'. Many try to cling to a positive view of their strengths but teasing about their weaknesses from their peers and a negative view of their abilities from others does little to help this attempt. This sets up a cycle of failure:

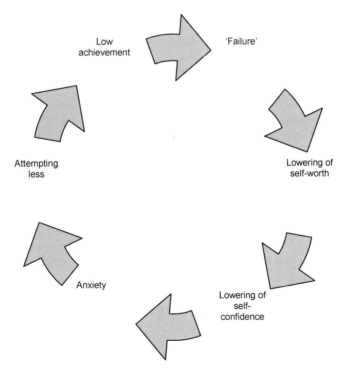

Figure 2 The cycle of failure

Lowered self-esteem can result in:

- Disruptive behaviour. The student may feel that he is seen as 'thick' so acts the idiot. He may also believe that disrupting lessons gives him 'status' among his peers. Dyslexic students can also become the 'class joker' or bully.
- Uncooperative behaviour. He may fear 'being wrong' and not answer questions or participate in discussions in class. This can be disastrous for the student who has difficulty recording his idea in writing but who has a good knowledge of his subject as there is little opportunity for the teacher to assess his ability and he may continue to believe that he 'knows nothing'.
- Using avoidance tactics. Many dyslexic students are extremely skilled in avoidance tactics and creative when making up excuses.
- Depression.
- Loss of motivation.
- Unwillingness to develop new skills or try new hobbies.
- Lack of ambition. He may lower his sights when considering career prospects.
- Inability to integrate fully in a social group. He may not feel 'as good as' other group members. He may not wish to give opinions for fear of being laughed at.
- Losing faith in his abilities. He will focus more and more on his 'failures' and lose sight of his strengths. It is not uncommon to point out a student's achievement only to be answered with a shrug of the shoulders.
- Feelings of underachievement. Underachievement is often measured in terms of educational benchmarks. This means that the gifted dyslexic student who achieves 7 'C' grades at GCSE will not be classified as underachieving. However, he will know that he has the intellectual capacity to gain 7 'A' grades and will feel that he has underachieved in relation to his potential. He also knows that this may have an effect on the course of his future studies and career.

Case studies

Dean was a very bright, creative Year 5 student whose dyslexia led to significant difficulties with reading, writing and spelling. His teacher had noticed that his erstwhile sunny disposition was rapidly disappearing and his mother reported a lack of enthusiasm for going to school. Dean admitted to his teacher that he believed that he was not working to the same standard as his peers and the constant reminder given by the displays of work around the class was causing a lowering of self-esteem. He could see that some students were filling whole sides of paper with writing while his contribution amounted to three or four lines. His teacher had believed that she had praised him for the quality rather than the content of his work but this had obviously not sufficed. Knowing Dean's creative strengths, the whole class were asked to illustrate their work to be displayed. Dean could now fill his piece of paper. The students were then asked to decide how they wished to display their work. Dean wrote a story about a magic box. He constructed a box, wrote the story on the faces of the box and decorated the box with the content of the story. This gained the admiration of his peers, teacher and the headteacher. These strategies proved to halt the downward spiral of his self-esteem and his teacher worked with a peripatetic specialist teacher to help Dean to develop further strategies to enable him to transfer to secondary education with greater self-confidence.

Susie's story is somewhat different. In science lessons, she completed practical experiments quickly and successfully and was an active participant in question and answer sessions. However, her literacy difficulties (not formally assessed at the time) led to very poor results in the Year 8 exams. Her teacher announced to the class that the result was 'the worst she had seen' and intimated that her practical success had resulted from copying friends' work. I met Susie as an adult and she stated that, although she had recognized that she struggled with literacy tasks, this one insensitive comment precipitated a lack of self-esteem which was also fuelled by a degree of teasing from her peers who were now more aware of her difficulties. She admitted that she began to 'give up' from that point and did not achieve for the remainder of her school career. Susie was in her mid-20s before she embarked on a course of further study, encouraged by her family and a supportive employer who recognized her strengths

Studies have shown that increase in self-esteem has led to increased understanding of information and learning strategies, achievement and involvement in classroom activities and discussion.

Helping to boost self-esteem

- The most important aspect is to avoid potentially damaging comments. 'You haven't written much' may seem like an innocuous statement of fact but the student may have heard the same statement several times that day. The teacher may also not be aware that she has said the same thing to the student on other occasions, but he will remember.
- Give praise for effort as well as achievement.
- Give praise *only* when it is due. It is very easy to want to praise the student who appears dispirited with his efforts but he will not appreciate genuine praise if he is under the impression that praise is given lightly or when it is unwarranted.
- Give tasks in small, achievable steps. The student will then feel that he has achieved more.
- Pair the student with another who is weaker in a particular activity so that he has the opportunity to exhibit his skills. This is particularly effective when the other student is a high achiever in other areas.
- Make the student feel that he is a valued member of the class. Ask his opinion or discuss a topic with him.
- Give 'constructive' criticism rather than negative remarks. Dupree (2005) suggests giving a 'feedback sandwich' in which constructive criticism is 'sandwiched' between two positive comments or praise for work.
- On a similar theme, I always start one-on-one lessons with an exercise that a student can achieve to encourage a positive start to the lesson and end with an achievable task so that the student can leave with a feeling of personal success.
- Subtle marking can help. Some teachers avoid giving crosses and replace these with a different shape. However, the student may come to associate that shape with failure as he did the crosses.
- Find a famous dyslexic individual who could act as a role model for the student. Many dyslexic sportsmen and women, musicians, actors and businessmen and women have been increasingly willing to share their experiences of dyslexia. The student may wish to read articles about the person but the simple knowledge that he or she has gained success in a particular field can be motivational.

- While it is recommended to encourage strengths and foster a positive outlook, it is easy to give the student unrealistic expectations. It is better to utilize strengths, interests and strategies for accommodating dyslexia productively to achieve personal success than to aim outside the parameters of ability and interest merely to 'prove a point'. This can perpetuate the belief that he has 'failed' yet again.
- Encourage the student to demonstrate his skills.

Case study

Sophia, a Year 5 student, struggled both academically and socially in her class. She was a gifted dancer and won awards in her out-of-school classes. Sophia was given the opportunity to show her awards and give a demonstration of her dancing in the whole-school assembly. Her self-esteem rose immediately, there was a marked difference in her relationships with her peers and her motivation for work improved.

Praise should be realistic. The dyslexic student will be far more appreciative of genuine, well-earned praise.

The need for assessment – identifying strengths and weaknesses

Most educational psychologists and specialist teachers will agree that the formal assessment leading to a diagnosis of dyslexia should be just one stage of an information-gathering process triggered by concerns that the student may exhibit signs of dyslexia. As recommendations in the report should be linked to teaching, the diagnosis should precipitate continuous assessment of the student's progress, in both learning and socio-emotional contexts.

Stages of assessment

Concerns may be raised by the parent or other family member, teacher, learning support assistant, members of other professional bodies (speech therapist, optometrist) and by the student himself. The concerns and frustration voiced by the younger student should always be taken seriously as this may be the first indication that all is not going smoothly. The Year 5 student who may not appear to be underperforming may still complain that he cannot write down all of his ideas. He may hate the fact that he sometimes cannot keep up with what the teacher is saying and has to ask his peers. Good communication between all those involved in the student's learning experience is essential although this may not always be easy to achieve, particularly in secondary school where several subject teachers will be involved in the student's learning experience and parents or carers may not be as easily accessible as they are in the primary sector.

Concerns should be gathered centrally, ideally by the Special Educational Needs Coordinator (SENCO) who can compile an initial profile of strengths and weaknesses from the evidence given to her.

A history of attainment scores should be included as evidence of a concern regarding the student's rate of progress.

A comparison between CAT scores (or other cognitive assessment scores) and attainment scores may be made to show evidence of a possible discrepancy between underlying ability and attainment.

The school may conduct group screening tests for reading, writing and spelling. In addition, a qualified teacher may wish to administer an individual dyslexia screening test such as:

- Dyslexia Early Screening Test Second Edition (DEST-2) for ages 4 years 6 months to 6 years 5 months.
- Dyslexia Screening Test – Junior (DST-J) for ages 6 years 6 months to 11 years 5 months.
- Dyslexia Screening Test – Secondary (DST-S) for ages 11 year 6 months to 16 years 5 months.

These and other assessment materials are available from Harcourt Assessment (see contacts list at the end of the book). Harcourt can advise on the use of these materials and the qualifications needed to administer tests.

Evidence of concerns regarding social and emotional issues should be included.

In addition to the list of concerns, the student's strengths must also be recognized to enable the most effective development of teaching strategies. The following should be considered and noted where appropriate:

- Learning styles – does he have strong visual, auditory or kinaesthetic skills? Does he use, or is encouraged to use, these as effectively as possible?
- Doe he excel in a particular subject – is he a talented sportsman, artist?
- Does he have good verbal communication skills?
- Is he adept at solving problems?
- Is he a creative thinker?
- Does he have good interpersonal skills?
- Is he developing independent strategies to accommodate his difficulties?
- Does he show determination and diligence in accommodating difficulties?

The last two are sometimes not considered when listing strengths but the ability and determination to face challenges in learning plays an important role in eventual success.

The continuous process of information gathering may lead to a decision that the student should have a formal assessment of his strengths and weaknesses which may or may not lead to a diagnosis of dyslexia or other specific learning difficulty. A paper or computer-based screening may give an indication that the student is 'at risk' of being dyslexic but a full diagnostic assessment requires the knowledge and skill of the trained assessor to give a complete picture of the student's profile or strengths and weaknesses.

> **Formal diagnostic assessment of dyslexia should be one stage of an ongoing process of assessment carried out by all of those involved in the learning and emotional experiences of the student.**

Interpreting the psychological assessment report

The educational psychologist or suitably qualified specialist teacher will combine the background information that she is given (or obtained herself from the student, parent and teacher) with assessment tests appropriate to the student's age. Different tests may be used by individual assessors but the information gathered in the following areas will be similar.

Underlying ability

Verbal and non-verbal (performance) ability. May be referred to as Verbal IQ and Visual IQ. Individual scores may be given for each or a 'general' score may be given. I prefer to give individual scores as there could be a marked difference in the scores which is evened out when they are combined.

Cognitive processing

- Auditory memory (memory of information delivered verbally).
- Visual memory (memory of information delivered visually; usually in the form of written words, pictures or symbols).
- Auditory processing (speed and accuracy of processing information delivered verbally).
- Visual processing (speed and accuracy of processing information delivered visually).
- Auditory discrimination (hearing differences between sounds).
- Visuomotor skills (hand–eye coordination).
- Sequencing (alphabet, days of the week, months of the year. May involve asking the student to 'find' a letter at random).
- Phonological awareness and processing (ability to identify, retrieve and manipulate the sounds of language).

Attainment

- Reading – single word recognition, non-word reading, text reading (oral and silent), comprehension, reading speed.
- Spelling – single word spelling, dictation of sentences.
- Free writing – speed, legibility, grammar, sentence structure, coherence of writing, vocabulary used.
- Numeracy – accuracy, speed, formative assessment of how a problem is tackled.

Other tests

These may include an Intuitive Overlay Test (screening for Meares-Irlen Syndrome – see Chapter 4) or tests/checklists for indicators of dyspraxia or Attention Deficit Disorder (ADD). The assessor can report the findings of these but will usually recommend referral to other professionals such as optometrists, GPs and occupational therapists for further assessment.

Scores may be given as follows:

- Most scores are normed scores which are age-related scores. This means that the student's scores are compared to those of individuals within the same age range.
- Standardized scores where the mean (average) is 100 and a standard deviation (either side of the mean into which 66 per cent of the population fits) is 15.
- WISC subtest score where the mean is 10 and a standard deviation is 3.
- Percentiles are given on a score of 1 to 100. A score at 65th percentile means that, out of a sample of 100 people within the same age range, the individual would achieve the same or higher score than 65 of that sample. The mean score is 50.
- Reading or spelling age. This gives the average age at which that score would be achieved.
- Some assessors will give a descriptor from a range; for example, lower extreme, well below average, below average, average, above average, well above average, upper extreme.

Results will be tabled or put in chart form to enable the reader to gain an overview of the student's strengths and weaknesses in the areas tested. Often, the dyslexic student exhibits a 'spiky' profile in which scores fall in more than one range. Often, a discrepancy between underlying ability and attainment scores will be seen. In these cases, there is a potential for the student's ability to be underestimated if he is judged on his written work rather than being allowed to exhibit his knowledge verbally. This can be extremely frustrating for the student. However, it is a common misconception that there will always be a discrepancy between these two areas in dyslexic students and this is not always the case.

A crucial aspect of the assessment is observation. The assessor will look at strategies the student uses to tackle the tests, behaviours and body language exhibited during the tests, learning styles deployed, signs of visual or physical discomfort or fatigue, and listen to comments made by the student. She may tactfully and gently question the student as to how the task was tackled (a student who made no attempts at guessing unfamiliar words when reading or spelling may not be unco-operative but have very poor phonological awareness skills).

The assessor will then use all of the various strands of information that she has gathered to arrive at and record her conclusions regarding the student's strengths and weaknesses and suggest recommendations for teaching and study. The report should link the identification of the difficulties with recommendations for intervention and classroom teaching strategies.

Grant (2004) states that a diagnostic report should be explanatory, transparent and insightful rather than merely being a certificate. I believe that the report should be an easily understood and informative working document that will enable all those involved to enhance the student's learning experience. Terminology should be explained or included in the text in such a way as to render it easily understood. Recommendations should be appropriate and achievable.

> The assessment report should be in accessible language giving a clear profile of the student's strengths and weaknesses and include recommendations for teaching and study.

2 Learning Styles

Learning styles and multisensory teaching

At the start of my specialist teaching career, a friend gave me a framed script which read 'If you can't learn the way I teach, can I teach the way you learn?', a paraphrase of Harry Chasty's observation. Hopefully, I no longer need the reminder but this question epitomises the crucial need to recognize the strengths, weaknesses and learning or thinking styles of all students and particularly the dyslexic student who may think differently.

In learning and in everyday life, information is absorbed and processed through three sensory channels – sight, hearing and touch/movement. As learning styles, these are labelled visual (seeing), auditory (hearing) and kinaesthetic (doing).

Consider an everyday task: you need to learn how to use a new DVD player at home. Your partner has already mastered this. Do you:

V) Read the instructions?
A) Ask your partner to read the instructions to you or tell you what to do?
K) Try to work it out by experimenting with the keypad?

If your answer is V but your partner decided to tell you how to operate the machine there is the distinct possibility that, after a short while, you will ask your partner to give you the instructions so that you could read them yourself. Your initial attempt at tackling the task was not carried out in a manner suited to your learning style and was, therefore, less successful. However, by asking for the instructions, you are showing an awareness of your own learning style and the ability to alter your method of learning accordingly.

The non-dyslexic learner may find learning a less enjoyable or effective experience when material is given or lessons are delivered in a style that does not match his learning style. Observe a science lesson in which the teacher demonstrates an experiment, reinforces this with a verbal explanation and asks the class to carry out a similar experiment. Some members of the class will be highly focused on watching the teacher carry out an experiment. Others will listen attentively to the explanation of the concept. A third group will be eager to get on with replicating the experiment themselves.

Multisensory teaching is effective for all students as the different styles of presentation will appeal to the learning styles of all members of the class. It is particularly beneficial to the dyslexic student as he can use those methods of delivery that suit his strengths to compensate for his areas of weakness. Many dyslexic students will have weaknesses in either auditory or visual memory and processing. A few will experience difficulty in both areas. In the example of the science lesson, the student with the weak visual sequential memory could still learn effectively by listening to the teacher and carrying out the experiment himself. If a concept were to be explained purely through verbal delivery, it is highly likely that the student with weak auditory memory or processing skills would gain little understanding.

Multisensory teaching methods are widely used in programmes for teaching dyslexic students. The student can use his strengths for efficient learning while practising skills that they are weaker at. Some find that learning through two channels simultaneously (for example reading a text while listening to a tape of the text) is beneficial.

In Chapter 1 it was suggested that the teacher look at her own hemispherical dominance. It is also an interesting exercise to investigate your learning style and reflect on the influence your learning style has on your teaching methods. As a specialist teacher, I am obviously an exponent of multisensory teaching. However, a teacher who attempts to deliver a lesson that is completely alien to her learning style may find that she does not enjoy the lesson and that it may actually be less effective.

Many dyslexic students learn compensatory strategies from an early age and can employ these successfully. Others may need support and instruction to help them to recognize their strengths and weaknesses and use this awareness in their learning. In either case, the student cannot use compensatory strategies if he is not given the opportunity to do so.

Recognizing learning styles – visual, auditory and kinaesthetic

- Ask the student how he is tackling a task. While carrying out the experiment himself during the aforementioned Science lesson, he may emphasize how what he saw, heard or is doing is influencing his method of working and learning. It is also helpful to consider the influence of hemispheric dominance (see Chapter 1). Is the student working in a sequential manner or taking a global view of the problem?
- Listen to the language the student uses. The visual learner would say 'I can see how that would work', the auditory learner 'I can hear what you are saying' and the kinaesthetic learner 'It doesn't feel right'.
- Watch behaviour in class. Look at which types of activity are carried out with greatest enthusiasm or success. Note the student who seems consistently demotivated when learning through a particular method. This is particularly important if the student has not had a diagnosis of dyslexia but concerns have been raised. This could act as further evidence of a weakness in a particular area.
- One of the findings from the 1970s studies of Bandler and Grinder was that eye movements reflect learning styles. I regularly use this theory during assessment when administering a Digit Span Test (an assessment of auditory sequential memory in which the student is given series of numbers which he has to repeat. The task becomes increasingly more difficult as the series increase in length). Put simply, if the student is looking up whilst remembering or processing information, he is a visual learner. If he is looking ahead or to the left or right, he is an auditory learner. If he looks down, he is a kinaesthetic learner. This can be carried out as a small group exercise with a prepared chart to record behaviours. I have also found that some students whose visual weaknesses mean that they rely quite heavily on auditory skills will verbally 'rehearse' the numbers. Some kinaesthetic learners will move their fingers sequentially while stating the numbers, as though the numbers are imprinted on them.
- Learning style questionnaires comprising a series of questions similar to those above are readily available on the internet (use a search engine such as Google). Some educational establishments in the post-compulsory sector are now routinely asking students to complete learning style questionnaires during the induction process. Many of the questionnaires can be used as a framework for the teacher to adapt to the age or interest of her students. One questionnaire that I used asked:

If you wanted to contact a friend would you prefer to :

a) go and see him
b) phone him
c) write to him.

My students would not have considered option c) as it would not be relevant to them so I amended it to c) text or email him.

Many people will find that their answers will be evenly spread across all three areas throughout the questionnaire with, probably, a slight preference for one style (a 9-5-6 result across 20 questions would not be uncommon). However, some dyslexic students may show a marked preference for or a marked avoidance of one particular style: one student, who was subsequently diagnosed as having very weak visual processing skills, recorded a score of visual 0, auditory 11 and kinaesthetic 9. This is a useful exercise for all students as the student who is not dyslexic may also exhibit a marked preference.

Multisensory activities

The following are examples of activities or methods of delivery that are effective for the visual, auditory or kinaesthetic learner. Most of the suggestions below will be usual practice for most teachers. However, matching delivery to the dyslexic student's learning style is essential.

Visual

- Use visual displays in the classroom – posters, wall displays.
- Introduce mind mapping or spidergrams. Students can incorporate pictorial representation.
- Use or encourage the student to use colour – pens, pencils, coloured whiteboard markers, colour-coded maps of school or coloured dividers for different topics.
- Include pictures, diagrams, symbols on worksheets, whiteboard demonstrations.
- Use video or DVD as teaching to demonstrate. If available, the student could use video or still photography to record his work.
- Give visual demonstration of concepts.
- Encourage the student to visualize information as an aid to memory.

Auditory

- Give verbal explanations.
- Reinforce visually presented information verbally.
- Use discussion, either in pairs or as a whole-class activity.
- Encourage the student to give explanations to others. Verbalizing his thoughts will aid memory.
- Use the media of poetry, music and drama.
- Use audio tapes. The student can listen to recorded versions of books.

He can record his thoughts or notes onto a dictaphone and use the recordings for revision.

Kinaesthetic

- Set up practical activities where possible.
- Allow the student to give practical demonstration rather than verbal explanation.
- Allow the student to present work that involves practical activity – modelling, making posters or displays, craft work.

- Use 3-D models and encourage exploration.
- Use tactile materials to aid memory. Alphabet letters made from wood, felt or carpet will appeal.
- Use dance and movement.
- Allow the student to doodle – he may be using doodling to encourage muscle memory.
- Where possible, allow the student to move around in class – a kinaesthetic learner may find difficulty in sitting still, listening and looking without doing anything physical. Using a stress ball or piece of plasticine can also help him to concentrate.
- The younger student may enjoy helping to clear up at the end of a lesson.
- During group work, the kinaesthetic learner could take on the role of writing down the group's findings, opinions, ideas.
- Use games such as board or card games, jigsaw puzzles. The kinaesthetic learner may like to create games for him or the class to use.

Thinking styles in mathematics

In addition to these learning styles, research has suggested that there are two distinct thinking styles in mathematics. Steve Chinn and his two American colleagues labelled these styles 'inchworm' and 'grasshopper'.

The following table illustrates the characteristics of each.

	Inchworm	Grasshopper
First approach to a problem	1. Focuses on the parts and details. 2. Looks at the numbers and facts to select a suitable formula or procedure.	1. Overviews, holistic, puts together. 2. Looks at the numbers and facts to estimate an answer, or narrow down the range of answers. Controlled exploration.
Solving the problem	3. Formula, procedure-oriented. 4. Constrained focus. Uses one method. 5. Works in serially ordered steps, usually forward. 6. Uses numbers exactly as given. 7. More comfortable with paper and pen. Documents method.	3. Answer-oriented. 4. Flexible focus. Uses a range of methods. 5. Often works backwards from a trial answer. 6. Adjusts, breaks down/builds up numbers to make an easier calculation. 7. Rarely documents method. Performs calculations mentally (and intuitively).
Checking and evaluating answers	8. Unlikely to check or evaluate answer. If a check is done it will be by the same procedure/method. 9. Often does not understand procedures or values of numbers. Works mechanically.	8. Likely to appraise and evaluate answer against original estimate. Checks by alternative method/ procedure. 9. Good understanding of number, method and relationships.

Source: *The Trouble With Maths (Chinn 2004)*

Figure 3 Thinking styles in maths

Chinn (2004) defines the two as:

> Grasshoppers are holistic, intuitive and resist documenting methods. Inchworms are formulaic, procedural, sequential and need to document.

Many students will have developed a thinking style which incorporates aspects of both. Others may use different styles to tackle different mathematical problems. Difficulties may lie ahead for those whose style sits firmly at the extremes of either inchworm or grasshopper. The grasshopper, who tends to simply write the answer to a problem rather than write down workings, may lose marks during examinations when marks are given for documentation of workings. If a sequence of procedures needs to be undertaken, it is very difficult for the grasshopper to 'back track' to find where an error has occurred. The inchworm may get 'bogged down' in detail and have insufficient time to finish an examination.

The greatest difficulty can be encountered by the dyslexic inchworm who will be formula- and procedure-oriented. If the student has a poor memory for formulae and number facts and slow processing speeds, it is easy to imagine that his experience of maths learning may be an arduous one if he is not encouraged to try to develop a degree of flexibility in his thinking.

Encouraging flexibility

The first consideration must be the teacher's own thinking style. Look at the table (Figure 2) and reflect on your own preferred method of tackling problems. During dyslexia awareness training, there is much animated discussion on this topic as, often, teachers have been unaware that they have been teaching to their own preferred style and not adapted their methods of delivery and use of resources to their students' styles.

Secondly, you will need to identify the students' thinking styles. One way is to encourage the student to explain his methods of working and discuss these with his peers. This has the dual effect of allowing you to gain an insight into how the student is thinking and also encourages students to share their methods (as suggested in the National Numeracy Strategy). This is also an ideal opportunity to reflect on whether you can integrate some of the learning strategies practised by the students into your teaching style. A word of warning – do not try to modify your teaching style beyond what is comfortable and workable for you.

As I regularly encounter new groups of students, I often use a very basic exercise during the first lesson to get an overview of thinking styles which will then be built on as my work with them progresses.

The students are asked to carry out a simple addition such as 35 + 26 (the sum is both written on the whiteboard and given verbally as a multisensory delivery) and to write the working out and answer on an individual whiteboard.

The inchworms are likely to give:

$$\begin{array}{r} 35 \\ 26\ + \\ \hline 61 \\ \hline 1 \end{array}$$

The grasshoppers are likely to give:

$30 + 20 = 50$
$5 + 6 = 11$
$50 + 11 = 61$

Or:

$40 + 30 = 70$
$5 + 4 = 9$
$70 - 9 = 61$

Or (despite being asked to show workings):

61

Make note of the inchworm who has difficulty in completing the task in the given time.

Chinn suggests that the different thinkers should adopt two basic characteristics of each other's styles:

Two key grasshopper skills an inchworm should adopt:
1. Inter-relating numbers, for example, seeing 9 as 1 less than 10, seeing 5 as half of 10.
2. Overviewing any problem, for example reading to the end before starting or getting a feel of what the answer may be.

Two key inchworm skills a grasshopper should adopt:
1. Explaining their methods
2. Documenting their methods.

Students should be encouraged to discuss their methods of tackling problems and reaching solutions, either as a whole-class exercise or through paired work. If a grasshopper can be paired with an inchworm, the two can learn a lot from each other.

Case studies

Nabil and Prashant were Year 6 pupils. Nabil's dyslexia caused difficulty with remembering number facts and times tables, sequential processing and reading. His maths attainment scores were low. Nabil had excellent verbal and non-verbal reasoning skills and proved to be adept at problem-solving exercises. Prashant was an 'intractable' inchworm. He could perform calculations far more complex than would be expected for a student of his age but had difficulty in 'seeing' problems. I was working with a small group of more able students on problems set on the NRICH maths enrichment website (www.nrich.maths.org.uk). Prashant was struggling to identify the processes needed to complete the problems. Despite his attainment results, Nabil was allowed to join the group and was allotted Prashant as his 'buddy'. Prashant read the questions, Nabil gave an overview of the problem and expected outcome, then Prashant demonstrated the processes and methods of calculation needed. The boys demonstrated an appreciation of the other's strengths and a patient attitude when explaining concepts that the other found difficult; qualities that were carried over to other areas of school life. The result of this pairing was an unbeatable success rate within the group and a marked increase in the levels of attainment and self-esteem of both boys.

However, practitioners in the field generally agree that some students are so entrenched in their styles that it is impossible to instigate change. Emma, a Year 9 student who had difficulty with the concept of estimation, would expend much time and effort during tests fully calculating answers to questions such as 'estimate 68.7 x 31.2'. Consequently, she gave the answer 2143.44. The correct answer should be 70 x 30 = 2100; the numbers are rounded up or down to the nearest 10. I witnessed the sterling work carried out by Emma, her maths teacher and support staff on this topic, apparently with success. However, when faced with this question again, her answer was 2143. She had still calculated the sum in full but had rounded the answer to a whole number. Emma was pleased with her efforts and the staff had to rethink their strategies.

When considering the characteristics of the right-brained dyslexic student, it could be assumed that many dyslexic students would be grasshoppers. However, their work with hundreds of dyslexic students has led Chinn and Ashcroft (1998) to believe that 'there are more inchworms than grasshoppers'.

3 The impact of dyslexia on literacy and communication skills

The next three chapters will examine the impact of dyslexia on verbal and written communication skills. The emphasis is on the impact within the classroom and offers some ideas for accommodating this in your teaching.

It may be helpful if the following are kept in mind:

- Ask the SENCO if you could read the diagnostic report to gain a clearer picture of the possible impact of students' dyslexia. It may only be necessary to read the conclusions of the report and recommendations if these are outlined separately.
- Not all students with dyslexia have been formally assessed by an educational psychologist or specialist teacher. The 'signs of dyslexia' section in Chapter 1 may help the teacher to identify students for whom there may be cause to consider the possibility of dyslexia. The examples shown in this chapter may also 'ring warning bells'. All concerns are likely to be welcomed by the school's SENCO, particularly at secondary level where it can be a more extensive task to obtain formative assessment due to the number of staff teaching the student and the varied skills needed for successful learning in each subject.
- Dyslexia can affect students in a wide variety of ways to varying degrees. Despite the student being taught by the same teacher in a specific subject area, dyslexia may still impact more markedly when different skills are needed.
- Difficulties of dyslexia can manifest at any time in the student's career. Reports from earlier years may not have identified causes for concern as these may not have shown at the time; teachers cannot miss signs that have not yet appeared. An explanation of this aspect of dyslexia may be helpful to parents who query the reasons for their child's 'late' diagnosis.
- The areas of difficulty may present in students who do not have dyslexia. They will still benefit from your use of these strategies.
- Strategies outlined in the next chapters are ideas that you may wish to adopt. It is not always possible, for logistical or financial reasons, to implement these ideas. Some may also not be suitable for, or be potentially detrimental to, students with other specific learning or physical difficulties (for example using coloured pens on whiteboards when a colour-blind student is a member of the class).
- Whilst it can be both stimulating for the teacher and productive for students if the teacher learns and incorporates different approaches in her teaching and adopts new strategies for learning, it can sometimes be counter-productive to use teaching styles and resources that she does not feel comfortable with.

Overview of potential difficulties

As stated in the British Dyslexia Association's definition (Chapter 1), dyslexia, in addition to affecting reading and spelling, can also impact on maths, musical notation, verbal communication and organization. Teachers, who may have received little training or have limited experience of the impact of dyslexia, have believed that the student will only experience difficulty with reading and spelling. Most have found that considering dyslexia in terms of communication has given a greater understanding of the broader range of potential areas of difficulty.

Figure 4 outlines the skills needed for effective verbal and written communication. It can easily be imagined that weaknesses in any of these skills can reduce the effectiveness of both or either of verbal or written communication.

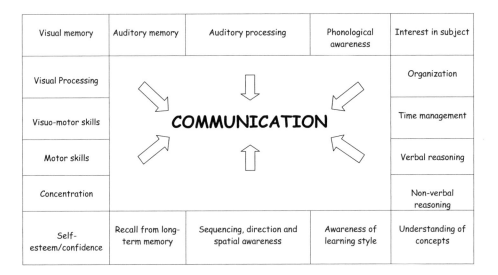

Figure 4 Skills needed for effective verbal and written communication

For those teachers who have an interest in the impact of dyslexia on music and art, the following are recommended:

Music and Dyslexia, Opening New Doors edited by Tim Miles and John Westcome. This is an anthology which combines the experiences of dyslexic musicians with contributions from teachers and researchers in the field.

'Including Dyslexics; Indicators of Dyslexia in Art Students' Drawings' is a fascinating paper by Qona Rankin, Howard Riley and Mary Davis. Although I believe that this research was based on the work of students in the post-compulsory sector, the findings are of interest to those teaching in the statutory sector, as are the references.

Case studies

Jon and Laura's situations resulted from lack of understanding of the impact of dyslexia on areas of study other than reading and spelling.

Jon had weak auditory short-term memory and processing skills and experienced difficulty in processing information and instructions delivered verbally. During practical technology lessons he constantly asked for repetition of instruction, was seen to be copying peers, missed stages of a procedure or simply did nothing. He was unable to repeat instructions given by the teacher. This was perceived as laziness, inattentiveness or disinclination to participate in the lesson. When the impact of Jon's difficulties were outlined to her, his teacher was visibly upset at her lack of recognition of the problem and, with advice from a specialist teacher, was able to put in place successful strategies to help Jon.

Laura was able to understand instructions and complete a practical task but, due to difficulties with word retrieval, she was unable to give an acceptable explanation of how she carried this out. Much of her work in one subject was carried out within a group and members of each group were expected to explain the processes of the work carried out. Consequently, her input in the task was underestimated as she could not, verbally, demonstrate understanding of the process and results. After Laura's difficulties were explained to the teacher, she was allowed to demonstrate her work, where possible, by giving practical demonstrations enhanced by brief explanations. Laura was also given 'advanced notice' that she would be expected to answer an imminent question. This allowed her time to think of what she intended to say.

Either scenario did not involve the written word but both had an adverse effect on the learning process and the ability to demonstrate knowledge. In both of these cases, teachers acting on specialist advice were able to modify their lessons to accommodate the needs of Jon and Laura without highlighting their difficulties to their peers.

Areas of impact

In this chapter, I will be examining eight areas where dyslexia may impact on literacy and communication skills. Each area will provide a theoretical perspective, a list of typical difficulties (illustrated by case studies where relevant) and suggested strategies for accommodating the needs of the student. As difficulties with reading and spelling can arise from one or more underlying weaknesses, strategies for reading and spelling will be discussed in Chapter 4.

Memory

Memory can be broadly subdivided into short-term, working and long-term memory.

Miller (1956) suggested that the short-term memory can hold, on average, seven facts. 'Miller's Magic Number' is 7 +/– 2 indicating that a 'normal' memory range would be between 5 and 9 items. The short-term memory acts as a holding area in which information can be briefly stored (up to 30 seconds) and repeated back as it was heard. The working memory processes the information to be stored in the long-term memory. Baddeley and Hitch (1974) produced the Model of Working Memory which divides this area of memory into three strands; the visuo-spatial sketch pad (which controls visual imagery), the phonological loop (rehearses verbal information) and the central executive (controls awareness of the information being assimilated). Earlier, Craik and Lockhart (1972) suggested that it was not the length of rehearsal of information nor the number of times that the information was processed that was important in transference from short-term to long-term memory but the manner in which this was transferred. Researchers who have taken this premise further have found that simply repeating information over and over may not be the most effective way of remembering.

These theories have major implications for the dyslexic student in both his learning and in everyday life as the transference of information may be inhibited if one of these strands does not contain all of the information that has been delivered to the students. A student may have been assessed as having a weak short-term auditory memory as he was able to recall only three items given verbally. If information is delivered verbally, his working memory will have just three items to process. If the same student has strong visual memory and can recall seven items given visually then it is likely that more information can be processed.

Many dyslexic students develop compensatory strategies from an early age. During assessment, a student with weak auditory memory skills can be observed looking at the ceiling during an auditory memory test as he is attempting to visualize the numbers to aid memory. Similarly, the student with weak visual memory will translate symbols or pictures into words which will be repeated. Some students may use muscle memory (the memory that every individual employs automatically to carry out everyday tasks such as walking and cleaning teeth) to help with the processing of new information. It may appear that the student is writing information for later reference but the physical act of writing can aid retention of information. One student could not remember people's names if he read them or was told them. If he wrote a name down, he could instantly recall it the next time he met the person.

When taking into account students' learning styles (see Chapter 2), the argument for delivering information in a multisensory format gathers strength, particularly for the dyslexic student. However, it is, again, crucial to remember that the student's perception of his preferred learning style may not match with strengths in his cognitive skills. He may also believe that there is 'one way to learn' a particular skill or topic and would not have contemplated using his ability to think differently. That is to say, the student who has poor auditory memory will not automatically have a preference for a visual learning style and may have to be helped to develop appropriate compensatory strategies.

Case study

Jansev, a Year 11 student, believed that she was a visual learner. She stated that she naturally responded more positively to demonstrations than verbal delivery of information. She excelled at art and had a creative visual imagination. Jansev needed to reread text frequently to gain comprehension, could not remember what she had read and found difficulty with revision. She was assessed as having a slow speed of visual processing. Discussion with Jansev elicited the fact that, when reading for pleasure, she would 'picture' events and keep an ongoing visual image to help her retain the thread of the story. Jansev was helped to develop this style in her studies and also became an avid user of mind maps.

Typical difficulties

- The student may forget 'strings' of instructions delivered verbally. This can be frustrating for the student both in study and in everyday life.
- Homework or equipment for the lesson may be forgotten.
- Instructions for homework, if given verbally, may be written down or remembered incorrectly.
- The student may appear to have only gained partial understanding of an explanation or appear to have 'the wrong end of the stick'. He may have forgotten part of what has been said and has tried to piece together what he has heard to make sense of the information. This may often happen with younger students who have a lesser amount of prior learning or experience to draw on.
- It may take longer for information to be processed into the long-term memory as this has to be done using smaller amounts of information.
- Students may suffer information overload during lengthy explanations which may lead to loss of concentration.
- The student may have difficulty in retrieving information quickly from memory.
- This can often manifest as difficulties with word retrieval in both written and verbal communication and may also be caused by weakness in processing. The student may say that the word is on the 'tip of his tongue' and may need to substitute a word that he can retrieve from memory. Students have reported that this can inhibit the fluency of writing or may not allow the student to use the most appropriate vocabulary. When this occurs during verbal communication, it can cause embarrassment, socially. The student may also be reluctant to answer questions or give explanations in class. The younger student may find particular difficulty as an immature vocabulary bank may limit the number of possible substitute words.
- Younger students will have difficulty with memory games. It has been practice, in the past, to play

games such as Kim's game which may involve the student having to remember up to nine items. Those students who find this difficult are encouraged to repeat the game. If the student has weak memory skills, no amount of practice at remembering large amounts of information will remedy his difficulties. There is also the very real danger, especially with the younger student who may be starting to realize that he has some difficulties, of instigating or fuelling his sense of 'failure'.

- Students of all ages may experience difficulty with learning the alphabet, days of the week, months of the year and other sequential information.
- The student may have difficulty in remembering the names of familiar people, places and objects. This can be an early indicator of dyslexia and should be noted by Early Years practitioners if this appears to be occurring regularly and causes frustration for the student.
- Younger students may have difficulty in remembering the words of songs and rhymes and may have difficulty in remembering actions to match songs.
- The student with auditory memory problems may have difficulty in learning new words and will need to see them written down before being able to remember them.
- When reading and spelling, the student with auditory memory problems may find difficulty in recalling the sound patterns to decode and build words even if they have previously demonstrated that they know and can apply the spelling rules.
- Spellings, even of commonly used words, may be spelled correctly one day and not the next. Students who have not been diagnosed as dyslexic could be deemed to be careless and told to check work. However, the student with poor visual memory may forget what a word looks like and may be unable to see his mistake.
- The student may need to reread text for meaning (this can also result from processing difficulties) as the student has forgotten what he has read at the start of the sentence. He may read a paragraph or page of text and be unable to remember much of the content.
- Students with insecure phonological awareness skills may read by sight reading or spell by remembering the look of a word. Weak visual memory skills may diminish the efficiency of this method of reading.
- Note-taking from speech can be an impossible task for many dyslexic students with auditory memory or processing problems.
- Similarly, for the student with a poor visual memory, copying from the board can be a slow exercise which can lead to inaccuracies or the inability to copy all information from the board. While his peers are remembering and copying several words or phrases at a time, the dyslexic student is likely to be copying single words. I have worked with students (particularly those whose spelling ability is very low) who have been unable to copy words and who have needed to refer back to the board for every single letter.

Strategies

- Where possible, deliver verbal information in 'chunks'. This could be interspersed with a question and answer or practical session. The key is to avoid information overload. If possible, give breaks in the middle of long lessons.
- Chunk verbal instructions.
- Give repetition where necessary. Importantly, encourage the student to ask the teacher (or his peers during discussion) for repetition. Many dyslexic adults still feel embarrassed to ask for repetition as they feel that it makes them 'look stupid' and it takes time for them to feel comfortable in doing so. Students who learn to ask at an early age do not develop this apprehension. It is also a good lesson in

- tolerance for their peers who will accept this as the norm for the particular student and exhibit patience.
- Where possible, explain topics in different ways as the student may be able to attach this to prior learning or experience.
- Teach songs and dance in small chunks, repeating each section as often as necessary before adding other verses or actions.
- Encourage the student to use visual, auditory or kinaesthetic 'pegs'. The 'Roman House' method works for some students. The student places words or ideas in 'rooms' in an imaginary house. He then pictures himself walking through the rooms and remembers information as he goes along. It may also help if the student attaches the information to an amusing idea. One Year 9 student pictured Sir Walter Raleigh wearing a ruff and cape, with a cigarette in one hand and a bag of chips in the other. This set the period and acted as a reminder of his better-known contributions to English culture.
- Where possible, employ multisensory teaching methods to facilitate retention of information by the student's stronger skills.
- Back up verbal information or instructions with notes on the whiteboard. Subject-specific vocabulary can cause a problem as the student may forget the word and substitute it with a similar-sounding word which will render the information inaccurate or unintelligible.
- Ensure that the student sees a written version of new vocabulary if auditory memory is weak.
- Ensure that the student has understood instructions and written them down correctly as he may misread, miscopy or mishear words.
- It may be necessary to write down instructions for the individual student with poor auditory memory. During PE lessons, instructions given verbally may have to be repeated.
- Homework diaries can be used to note equipment needed for the next lesson. Have spare equipment available should this system not work.
- Ensure that all instructions and information needed to complete homework are fully understood and written down. It may not be possible for the teacher to carry out this recommendation if she has more than one dyslexic student within the class. She may need to request support in the classroom if students are unable accurately or fully to complete homework due to this problem.
- Avoid giving lengthy written instructions to students with weak visual memory skills. Chunk or bullet-point instructions.
- Many teachers will place students with concentration problems at the front of the class. Research has shown that noise or distraction coming from behind an individual is far more distracting than that between the individual and the speaker.
- Allow the student with word retrieval problems time to give his answer. Subtle prompting may help but it is not always advisable to rush to supply a word as this will highlight the difficulty in class, possibly exacerbating a low self-esteem and adding to the reluctance to participate orally in class. Allow students to refer to text books or notes for subject-specific vocabulary. If the student knows in advance that he will be expected to talk about his work, he can be encouraged to make bullet-point notes or put subject-specific vocabulary on cards as reference.
- Have patience with the student who has word retrieval problems and discourage any adverse comments or body language from other students. Foster a tolerant atmosphere amongst all students.
- Encourage the use of mnemonics to aid memory. These can include pictures. Students should be encouraged to devise their own mnemonics, as this can often be more effective as a memory aid.
- Encourage students to chunk lists of objects, or information to be remembered, into smaller groups.

Case study

Harry and Luigi, both Year 5 students had been perceived by their class teacher as having difficulties with memory. Kim's game and 'I went to market and bought . . .' were not successful. Harry and Luigi were given a shopping list of nine items to remember which, of course, they could not do. The items were then divided, by me, into three groups: meat, vegetables and household items. Eight out of nine items were remembered. The following week, nine items were given but Harry and Luigi decided how these were to be grouped. A 100 per cent success rate was achieved. Interestingly, Harry closed his eyes during this session. When asked why, he explained that he was visualizing himself walking down his local high street and visiting the shops. Kim's game was successfully repeated with the students deciding how to group the objects. 'I went to market . . .' was played accompanied by actions suggesting the words. None of us forgot 'kangaroo'.

Harry and Luigi were encouraged to incorporate strategies for chunking information into their classroom lessons with the support of their class teacher who decided to adopt these as whole-class exercises.

Processing

Visual processing

Stein and Walsh (1997) cite Galaburda's post-mortem research into five dyslexic brains (which found that the magnocells were 20 per cent smaller than in control brains), their research and the research of others to conclude that impaired magnocellular visual function may affect reading and that 'one can be fairly confident that many dyslexics do have a fundamental impairment of their visual processing'. The paper 'To see but not to read; the magnocellular theory of dyslexia' discusses other aspects of dyslexia and is available on several sites on the internet. Weakness in this area can affect the speed and accuracy of interpreting written material and other information presented in visual form (diagrams, pictorial representation).

Case study

Tom was a mature student who had been a frequent non-attender at school and had not had a diagnosis of dyslexia. At college, he was diagnosed as having poor visual processing skills, average phonological processing skills and above average auditory memory and processing skills. His underlying ability scores were in the upper extreme range and his attainment scores were in the lower extreme range. He could not read his own name. During his first one-on-one support lesson, he was working on an assignment which required him to answer questions based on information found on a worksheet. He asked the tutor to read the whole of the worksheet, which was closely typed and contained complex information and subject-specific vocabulary, followed by the first question. To her amazement, he was able to answer the question without further reading of the text, indicating exceedingly strong auditory memory and processing skills. He was subsequently given a dictaphone to record lessons, written material was recorded and he received the services of a reader during examinations.

Auditory processing

Tallal et al. studied two groups of young students: one with language learning impairments and a control group of children of similar age and intelligence who did not present with language difficulties. They discovered that the first group took hundreds of milliseconds to process and discriminate between the acoustic features of sounds whereas children in the second group only took tens of milliseconds to complete the same tasks. This means, simply, that the first group took significantly longer to process sound.

The effect of a slow speed of processing sound on listening and speaking is an important consideration. It follows that if a student processes sounds at a slower speed than they are spoken, then he may easily lose track of an explanation or conversation. Fluent speech depends on the ability to recall accurately sounds and words at incredibly high speeds. Difficulties in this area can have significant implications for verbal communication within the classroom. The teacher may deliver a perfect explanation of a concept which may be lost to the student if the delivery is too fast. The student may have difficulty in verbally expressing his ideas fluently or accurately. He may not be able to keep pace with the speed and amount of information delivered during a group discussion, especially if more than one student is speaking at one time and could have difficulty in participating verbally in animated discussion.

Weakness in this area may also impact on the student's acquisition of sound phonological skills and, consequently, the auditory decoding skills necessary for reading and spelling.

Case study

Jodie, a Year 3 student, appeared to lack concentration during lessons and needed frequent explanations of concepts. She also exhibited aggressive behaviour towards her peers in the playground and would disrupt conversations. Her parents stated that they had no problems with behaviour in their interactions with her but noticed that she quickly became bored when watching children's television programmes with her sister. Her teacher observed her watching an educational video set in Africa. Jodie appeared to lack interest until she watched something that caught her attention visually such as a mother elephant and her baby. Her teacher realized that she had not been able to follow the dialogue in the programme. She was then observed in the playground by teachers and midday supervisors where it quickly became obvious that she could not keep up with her friends' conversations, particularly when this became animated or more than one student was speaking at the same time. She did not have the maturity to cope with the resultant frustration and so became disruptive and aggressive. Her parents had not encountered this as they had automatically paced conversations to her speed of listening and speaking. Jodie was referred to a speech and language therapist and showed marked improvement although she was later diagnosed as dyslexic.

> **The work of many researchers has indicated that a significant proportion of dyslexic individuals will have auditory or visual processing difficulties.**

Typical difficulties

- A reduction in the speed of word processing can slow down the decoding of words and hinder the flow of reading, thus disrupting comprehension which could lead to the need to reread information.
- Many students state that they do not read for pleasure as they can easily lose track of a plot.
- Others dislike reading aloud.
- The student may not be able to keep up with the pace of reading required from text or the blackboard.
- The student may have difficulty in keeping up with verbal delivery of instructions or information. He could lose the gist of an explanation which would result in misinterpretation or may 'switch off' completely.
- The student may not be able to participate fully in group discussion or retain information discussed.
- Slow speed of processing can affect the ability to interpret sentences or questions accurately and quickly or organize ideas, especially under timed conditions such as examinations.
- The student, due to slow speed of working, may produce quality or quantity of work, but cannot do both. They may fail to meet deadlines or complete work, especially under timed conditions in class or during examinations.
- Auditory processing problems, as well as memory difficulties, can affect word retrieval. In addition to the slow speed of retrieval of a word, the student may use Spoonerisms or a completely different word. A student asked her friend for some 'crocodile' instead of 'chocolate'.
- Processing can also affect the ability to organize ideas which can impact on the planning and structure of work. It is common to hear students comment on the difficulty that they have in getting thoughts onto paper. One student described this evocatively as 'a black hole between my brain and the paper'.

- A weakness in processing can affect concentration, particularly when the brain is 'overloaded' with information that it is trying to process. One student stated that he 'needed to concentrate on concentrating'.

Strategies

> The crucial element of any strategy to accommodate the needs of the student with auditory or visual processing difficulties is time; to process information, retrieve words, information and ideas and to record work.

- Where possible the teacher can attempt to pace the delivery of lessons to suit the needs of the student. As with Jodie's parents, this can quickly become automatic.
- Repeat instructions and information where necessary and encourage the student to ask for repetition.
- Allow the student extra time for reading activities in the classroom. This includes work on the board. Many students go home with half-completed notes or homework instructions because they do not tell the teacher that they have not finished copying from the board. Check that he has written all information needed to complete homework.
- Where possible, give breaks to allow for processing and retention of information. The student may appear to be daydreaming when reading but he may be subconsciously stopping to avoid information overload.
- Check that the student has correctly understood all instructions delivered verbally.
- It has been suggested that homework is written on the board at the start of the lesson to allow the student sufficient time to copy it rather than rushing at the end of the lesson. This strategy has been rejected by some teachers who have found that some members of a class will merely concentrate on those parts of the lesson that are needed to complete homework.
- Have patience with the student who may have problems with word retrieval (see 'Memory' section).
- A sympathetic view should be taken if the student does not produce the same quantity of work as his peers, particularly in the classroom. He may be able to produce an equivalent amount for homework as it is likely that he will work twice as long as his peers at home. When I am aware that this has happened, I will let the student know (without patronizing him) that I recognize the effort that he has expended.
- The student may qualify for extra time during examinations. Check with the SENCO or exams officer to see if this access arrangement is in place. If not, express your concerns to the SENCO who will judge whether screening and assessment for access arrangements will be appropriate.

Phonological awareness and processing

Phonological processing involves the use of the knowledge of sounds relating to the different letters of the alphabet and the patterns of blends and digraphs in processing written and oral language.

When it is considered that the English language is made up of 26 letters which, singly and in combination, produce a total of 44 sounds, it can be appreciated that the student who has insecure phonological processing skills has an uphill task with regard to reading and spelling. If the student does not have the ability to identify or manipulate sounds, it can slow down his ability to work out sounds within words and reduce the development of an automatic response when reading or spelling.

Wagner, Torgesen and Rashotte (in the Comprehensive Test of Phonological Processing examiner's manual) state that three distinct but correlated types of processing are involved in reading and writing. Phonological awareness is the awareness of and ability to access the sound structure of a language. Phonological memory is the temporary storage of phonological information in the short-term or working memory. Rapid naming of a series of letters or digits presented visually involves the efficient retrieval of phonological information from the individual's long-term memory as, although this also taps visual processing, the 'name' of the digit or letter must also be recalled and spoken at speed.

Bowers and Wolfe (1993) found that individuals who had deficits in both phonological awareness and rapid naming appeared to experience a greater degree of difficulty in reading than those who only had a deficit in one of those areas.

Vellutino and Scanlon (1991) showed that 83 per cent of participants in a retrospective analysis of several hundred impaired readers were deficient in mapping alphabetical symbols to sound.

> There is a large body of work that concludes that phonological deficits can be the cause of difficulties with reading and spelling for many dyslexic individuals.

Tests used in a diagnostic assessment may vary but will examine such areas as the ability to retrieve accurately, fluently and quickly the sounds of letters, segment words, delete letters or sounds from words, build words from given sounds, repeat non-words, recognize and produce rhyme. The assessment should give an indication of the nature of the difficulties that the student is experiencing and recommendations for teaching.

Many students will exhibit early signs of weakness in this area:

- Difficulty in synthesizing individual sounds to make words (c-a-t).
- Difficulty in learning or producing rhymes (man, can, ran).
- Mispronouncing words or mixing words (patercillar for caterpillar). Most young children will do this but could be a cause for concern if this persists or appears to the parent or Early Years practitioner to occur more frequently than would be expected.
- Slow recall of individual sounds.
- Cannot write letters if they are dictated individually.

- Cannot pick out letters from an alphabet tray or the board if given the sound.

The following may become obvious as the student progresses through Key Stages 2, 3 and 4:

- Difficulty in decoding when reading. May not be able to segment.
- Difficulty in building words phonetically.
- Misreads words for similar looking ones and cannot check by decoding.
- Will substitute similar looking words when spelling (pester for pasta).
- May produce 'bizarre' spellings (ktencli for kitchen – the student tried to visualize the letters) and cannot recognize or correct errors.
- Reading and spelling may be a slow process.
- Writes dictated spellings incorrectly even if sounds have been delivered slowly.

Strategies for verbal communication

- Introduce the concept of rhyme by pointing out words that rhyme when singing nursery rhymes. Encourage the younger student to do this.
- Recognition of rhyme can be an ongoing exercise in which the student is encouraged to find other words that 'sound the same'.
- Avoid telling the younger student that he is 'wrong' when words are mispronounced. Instead, give the correct pronunciation of the word and encourage the student to repeat it.
- Older students can play 'I-Spy' to help with recognition of initial sounds.

These difficulties can lead to a reduction in the speed of reading due to slow decoding speeds or the necessity to reread sentences when words have been misread. This can, in turn, lead to reluctance to read from a very early age and it is often difficult to change this attitude, particularly as the difficulty is likely to persist.

The student, particularly one who possesses a good verbal vocabulary, may use contextual clues to 'guess' a word rather than try to decode it. This will allow the student more fluency in his reading but can lead to misinterpretation of a sentence if he has wrongly predicted the word.

There could be serious consequences if this situation occurs during examinations; if the student misreads a word but his substitution could still make sense within the context of the text, or if he misreads a term that he is asked to define, he could easily give an incorrect answer or write an essay on a completely different topic to that given in the exam. He may also not have sufficient time to finish an examination.

The student may be reluctant to attempt spellings that he assumes he will misspell and will use those which he can spell. If this significantly limits his written vocabulary it could affect the quality or fluidity of his writing and the ability to demonstrate fully his abilities in creative thinking or knowledge of his subjects. We return to the student who may wish to write 'the exquisite Siamese reclined on the

Persian rug' and writes 'the cat sat on the mat'. A subject teacher may judge the student on the content of his writing (particularly if he does not participate verbally in class). This may have a detrimental effect on marks in examinations, especially if he also expends a significant amount of time on spelling which renders him unable to finish questions.

However, the ability of the dyslexic student to compensate for weaknesses, often without realizing he is doing so, can mask problems as the following cases clearly show.

Case studies

Stefan undertook an assessment for dyslexia in Year 10. His Form Tutor reported that he was articulate and possessed a broad verbal vocabulary. His school attainment assessments indicated that his reading and spelling ability had been average for his age until Year 8 and his general performance gave no cause for concern. In Year 9, these scores recorded as average but were in the lower end of the range. His English and history teachers had commented that the complexity of his written work did not appear to match that of his verbal ability. His science teacher had noted an increase in the incorrect use of terminology. Observation during the assessment noted that, while Stefan achieved an average score for reading and spelling, he was unable to attempt to read or spell unfamiliar words. Phonological awareness tests indicated that these skills fell in the 'lower extreme' range. Stefan could confidently recite the alphabet but could not give the sound of any letters and was not able to manipulate sounds. Throughout his school career, Stefan had used his stronger visual memory skills to read by sight recognition. An increase in the amount and complexity of vocabulary that he was now encountering, including subject-specific vocabulary, meant that he was experiencing memory overload. His inability to decode or build words did not allow him to check accuracy in reading or spelling. Consequently, errors in reading were being made more frequently. He was unable to use the full range of his vocabulary when writing as he was unable to 'work out' spellings that he could not remember. Stefan undertook an intensive phonics course with some degree of success and other strategies such as a personal dictionary and the use of a computer with spell-check facility were deployed to help with his studies.

In Reception and Year 1 Craig omitted all vowels from words when writing. This problem disappeared during Year 2 and it was thought that he had 'caught up' with the concept of phonics. By Year 8, he was exhibiting signs of dyslexia and an assessment revealed, among other things, insecure phonological skills and highlighted his inability to accurately identify and give the sound of the vowel sounds. Conversation with Craig elicited the fact that, when younger, he could not identify the correct vowel to use when spelling so, rather than 'get it wrong' he felt it safer to omit it. The problem had apparently 'disappeared' as he began to read words orthographically.

Suggested further reading:

Dyslexia, Speech and Language: A Practitioner's Handbook by Margaret Snowling and Joy Stackhouse.

Reading and Spelling: Development and Disorder. An anthology edited by R. Malateshi Joshi and Charles Hulme.

Sequencing

Difficulties with sequencing are often thought simply to involve basic sequential information such as learning the alphabet and times tables. However, problems with sequencing information can be lifelong and impact on many areas of learning.

Typical difficulties

- Sequencing difficulties affect spelling ability, the construction of sentences and speed when finding items in a sequence such as an alphabetical index. This can reduce the flow and hinder speed of working.
- Some dyslexic students may never be able to sequence fluently the days of the week, months of the year and the alphabet. A significant proportion of adult dyslexic students can recite the alphabet but need to work through the whole alphabet to find the position of a letter.
- Letters or syllables may be transposed or mixed up (potato becomes potota) and the student who also has weak visual memory or phonological awareness skills may not be able to recognize the error.
- The student may find difficulty with sentence structure or with ordering ideas in an essay resulting in work that may contain non-sequiturs or lack fluency. One student described this as 'like lottery balls. All of the words are in my head but I haven't got a clue in which order they will come out'.
- The student may have difficulty in following a sequence of instructions. In practical sessions this could render errors irreversible or be a potential safety issue. Backtracking to rejoin a sequence is also time consuming. The student could be accused of taking insufficient care or interest in the task.
- He may also lose track of the content of a lesson.
- The student may get lost during processes in science or maths.
- He may also have difficulty with sequencing information. This could impact on the presentation and memorizing of information in history and geography and the sequence of events in a novel.

Strategies

- Younger students can sequence the alphabet using wooden or plastic letters laid out in a rainbow shape. Hornsby, Shear and Pool (1999) suggest that the first seven letters are taught followed by the next nine and the final ten. Rhymes for days of the week and months of the year (Monday's child is fair of face) may also help.
- A letter can be removed from the rainbow and the student asked to replace it. He will be guided to the

correct place by the gap but this multisensory exercise will act as reinforcement of the order of the letters. Most young students enjoy this 'game' as it usually ends in success. The gap can be closed when it is felt that this exercise can be extended. This can be done as a whole-class exercise. Students can work in pairs to build the rainbow with models given where necessary and can take turns to remove letters and self-check the correct placement of letters.

- Where possible, instructions should be written to give the student a visual guide to follow. The student with sequencing problems who finds difficulty in remembering the sequences of procedures and processes, even those that are used often, may always need a model to follow.
- Instructions can be presented as flow charts to give a clearer picture of the order of processing.
- Sequences of events can be written on separate cards. These can be numbered or physically strung together (particularly useful if the student has difficulty with organization and may lose some of the cards).
- The student may wish to storyboard such information as historical events, geological tables or the story line of a novel to help with revision.
- Encourage the student to visualize a sequence. The student can imagine the characters in a novel enacting the sequence of events. He can visualize practical demonstrations given by the teacher or experiments that he has carried out.
- Different colours could be used in a similar way. Students have found that the use of colour prevents the repetition of stages but may not prevent stages being missed.
- Many students have stated that they prefer stages to be numbered.
- It is also effective if students cross out completed stages of work. This stops repetition and clearly reminds the student which stage they should be working on.

Direction

Directional difficulties can present the student with lifelong problems from using knives and forks correctly and playing games (many young students rarely win a game of 'Simon says') to map reading and giving or receiving directions. This is another area in which the impact on study may not be fully appreciated.

Typical difficulties

- Many dyslexic individuals confuse left and right. Some may also confuse forwards and backwards, up and down and directions on a compass.
- Students have related a dread of participating in sports due to the embarrassment caused if they run or throw a ball in a different direction to that instructed or bump into their peers.
- Instructions and tasks involving direction occur in many subject areas. ICT will involve left and right clicking of the mouse, map reading and coordinates appear in geography, directions for left and right hand will be given when playing a musical instrument, design and technology may involve direction, and maths computation and concepts require the ability to recognize direction.
- Reversing or inverting letters when writing or misreading letters such as 'b' for 'd' can arise from problems with direction.

- Younger students may begin reading or writing from right to left (I taught a Year 10 student who confided that she still needed to think where to start before reading and writing).

Strategies

- Some dyslexic individuals will write the letters 'l' and 'r' on their hands when they believe that they may be called upon to follow instructions. However, this strategy can be obvious to others and some students may not feel comfortable with displaying difficulties in this area.
- A more subtle reminder is to make an 'L' shape with the left hand (this may not work for students who regularly reverse letters) thus:

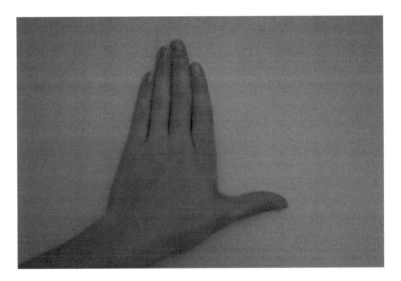

Figure 5 'L' hand

- The teacher can model practical examples for the student to follow. In such areas as dance routines and playing instruments this could be done as a mirror image.
- The student can be asked to move towards a particular person, object or area of the room rather than in a particular direction.
- The student can be encouraged to refer to compasses for reference.
- Equipment (including computer mouse) can be labelled. Sticky dots in different colours can be used to indicate left and right but care must be taken to ensure that the student remembers the corresponding colours.

Organization and time management

Problems with organization can be first noticed in students of all ages. The younger student who seems to find it impossible to keep his personal drawer tidy may be exhibiting early signs of dyslexia. A Key Stage 3 and 4 teacher once said that she could recognize the dyslexic student at the end of a break period as he would be the last one in the playground desperately searching through a disorganized backpack to find where he should be going next.

The older student may find increasing difficulty in organizing ideas on paper as higher level study skills are introduced. University students undergoing assessment have often commented that, in retrospect, they realized that difficulties with planning and structuring work had been increasing throughout their secondary school careers. In many cases, this has been a gradual process which the student and his teacher have judged to have resulted from an increase in the complexity of the work; a challenge that most of the student's peers will face. However, the dyslexic students comment that, despite possessing a good knowledge of the subject, having a wealth of ideas to express and knowing the principles of structuring and planning work, putting this into practice can prove problematic. In many cases, the student feels frustrated by his perception that his submitted work does not reflect his true abilities. Concerns have been expressed by students that these difficulties may have led to lower grades during examination.

Difficulties with time management can cause a great deal of frustration for the student and the teacher and is often mistaken for laziness or a careless attitude.

Typical difficulties

- Organizing ideas on paper. This can include difficulties with structuring sentences or complete essays. Essays may not be fluent, may contain irrelevant information or lack essential information (despite the fact that the student has demonstrated knowledge verbally) and may be illogically structured.
- The student may have difficulty in 'knowing where to start'. This can be very time consuming and frustrating during homework or class tasks but could have a major impact on examination results.
- The student may have difficulty judging the passage of time. When given 20 minutes to complete a task in class, he may only be half-way through at the end of that time.
- The student may not be able to simplify or précis text.
- He may not be able to multitask.
- There may be difficulties with time management affecting studies, planning work and simply managing to be in the right place at the right time. The dyslexic student may be the one who arrives late for class or after-school activities because they have gone to the wrong room or lost track of time during breaks. Difficulty in finding the correct equipment in the mornings can cause him to be late for school.
- Homework deadlines may not be met. The student may not be able to pace his homework and find that work is completed at the last minute or that he has too many pieces of homework to complete in one evening
- Work that has been painstakingly completed may be easily lost.
- Planning longer projects, assignments and coursework can prove difficult as the student may not be able to apportion the number of words, amount of time or degree of research needed for each section of the assignment. It is often thought that these difficulties will affect students at Key Stages 3 and 4

but Key Stage 2 teachers should be aware of the student who regularly rushes the last stages of ongoing projects after having spent an inordinate amount of time on one section of the project. Planning work in this way is a skill that students who are not dyslexic may also take time to develop, but if the student does not appear to 'learn' from the experience or exhibits other possible signs of dyslexia, this could be added to the list of evidence of cause for concern.

- Disorganized bags, trays, desks, folders often belong to the dyslexic student.

Strategies

- Check that instructions are written in homework diaries in the correct place – poor organizational skills often lead to the student writing work in random places. Consequently, he will not be able to find homework instructions. Diaries can record lists of textbooks and homework to bring to each lesson.
- Use charts for planning work, particularly when longer projects are being undertaken. This exercise can be carried in the classroom, with the help of a support assistant, if available. Enlist the support of parents to help the student to develop this strategy with a view to this becoming his independent way of working. It may be helpful if, initially, it is possible to give assignments in smaller chunks.
- When giving timed work in class, remind the student at regular intervals of the amount of time left.
- Routine is helpful although many dyslexic students will still arrive at the wrong room at the very end of the academic year.
- New students to the school may require a map with areas of the school colour-coded. Timetables can be similarly colour-coded to match the maps. It helps if the student has a copy in his bag, at home, in his locker and his form tutor has a copy in the event of him losing or forgetting any of these.
- Homework diaries can also be colour-coded using different colours for different subjects for easy reference to particular subjects.
- The student should be encouraged to develop ways to help him to organize work. Folders can include dividers and plastic pockets.
- Ensure that all work, clothing and equipment are named. Dyslexic students can spend many hours of their lives searching for lost property.
- Parents can ensure that bags and equipment are checked and packed correctly in the evening which prevents lost time and frayed tempers in the mornings.
- The older student who has a tendency to lose work may find that recording work on a computer may help although he should be encouraged to organize his work in folders to prevent time wasted searching through a multitude of files.

Motor Skills

Motor skills can be subdivided into 'gross motor skills' and 'fine motor skills'.

Gross motor skills activities involve using arms, legs and whole bodies for 'bigger' movements such as catching, throwing and kicking balls and riding bicycles.

Fine motor skills usually denotes those activities using fingers and hands and is applied to 'smaller' or 'intricate' activities such as writing, drawing and tying shoelaces.

Difficulties with coordination, fine and gross motor skills are most often associated with dyspraxia but, as discussed in Chapter 1, signs typical of one specific learning difficulty can overlap with other specific learning difficulties.

Studies vary as to the incidence of poor motor skills in dyslexic individuals but conclusions have been drawn that not all students with dyslexia may experience problems with motor skills (Ramus, Frith and Pidgeon 2002). The numbers of dyslexic students in colleges of art and famous dyslexic sportsmen and women appear to act as testaments to these findings.

However, for some students, the impact of poor fine motor skills in areas such as handwriting can be significant. In her chapter on handwriting in *How to Detect and Manage Dyslexia*, Philomena Ott quotes part of an open letter to the British Dyslexia Association written by Professor Peter Fellgett (1986): 'writing for me has always been laborious; I simply do not go onto autopilot. I believe that it is essential that teachers should understand that, what is a reflex to some people, is an explicit task for the dyslexic, and requires specific time for its execution.'

Case study

When Maria started Year 6, it was decided to give her handwriting exercises as her work was becoming increasing difficult to interpret. Maria concentrated and copied the exercises in a beautifully formed cursive script but this took her far longer than would be expected of a student of her age. When completing written work in class, she reverted to her barely legible writing. In addition, she had problems with spelling although made fewer errors in her weekly spelling tests than in her creative writing pieces. Spelling and handwriting were sacrificed in the rush to get her ideas onto paper. Maria was helped to develop planning strategies to produce drafts of her ideas in the hope that this would enable her to concentrate on spelling and writing in the final copy of her work. She continued with handwriting practice. Throughout Year 6, these strategies appeared to be successful but I met her again when she was a Year 11 student and she told me that, as spelling and the structure of sentences and essays had become more complex, her writing was slow and often illegible which had a detrimental effect on the fluency and quantity of her writing. She had often been unable to read notes that she had taken in class and had been assessed as needing to use a word processor in class and during examinations.

Typical difficulties involving gross motor skills

- PE and sports involving balls, apparatus. Throwing, catching and kicking balls will prove problematic. The student may 'misjudge' where he is when using apparatus.
- Bumping into people and objects. Note the student who is always walking into door frames even when there is a clear path to the door.

- Knocking things over. It is also common for items to be placed too near the edge of a table causing them to fall.
- Inability to ride a bicycle.
- The younger student may have difficulty in keeping his place or time when dancing or clapping.

Typical difficulties involving fine motor skills

- Handwriting may be poorly formed. This may also be a slow and arduous task. The student may have difficulty in writing in a straight line. He may start lines a little further in each time so that a paragraph may look like this:

> Humpty Dumpty sat on a wall
>   Humpty Dumpty had a great fall
>   All the king's horses and all the king's men
>   Couldn't put Humpty together again.

- Difficulty with using scissors. Model-making, craftwork or needle work may also cause frustration, particularly when the student has creative ideas that he struggles to reproduce. The younger student may feel frustrated if his peers are making more intricate models or can more easily manipulate smaller pieces such as Lego rather than Duplo.
- Using a knife and fork.
- Tying shoelaces and doing up buttons. Difficulty in tying shoelaces may not purely be an indicator of poor motor skills. The student may not have been able to remember the sequence of processes needed to accomplish this task.
- The younger student may not be able to tidy shelves neatly when asked.

Strategies

- The student may need to be referred for occupational therapy if significant difficulty with motor skills is identified.
- Take a sympathetic approach during sports and discourage teasing from other students.
- Velcro fasteners have been an invaluable alternative to shoe laces. Pre-knotted ties with elastic loops can help with getting dressed after games. Dyslexic adults have reported that they continue to buy elasticated ties, slip-on shoes and ask partners to do up buttons and fasten necklaces and cuff links.
- If the younger student is having difficulty with cutting food at lunchtime, offer to help. His parents can help him with practice in the privacy of his own home.
- Practise writing individual letters in sand or in the air with fingers. When tracing letters 'think big' at first and gradually reduce the size of the letters. Encourage the younger student to describe what he is doing, using imagery when appropriate (curly caterpillars, slithering snakes and kicking 'k'). These activities will all help to reinforce muscle memory.
- Encourage younger students to experiment with clay, sand, building blocks, paints, play-dough and other craft materials in the classroom. This will help to develop dexterity.
- Frequent practice of drawing and tracing shapes and letters, either with pencil or fingers will encourage the retention of those symbols through muscle memory.

- The National Literacy Strategy (2001) states 'children who have experienced the multisensory approach to learning letter shapes are less likely to develop bad handwriting habits'.
- Use lined paper for writing. Allow the student to choose a pen or pencil that is comfortable for him to use.
- There are now many types of writing aids available that are appropriate for all ages of students, including pen and pencil grips, triangular pencils, easy grip pens, finger-grip rulers and writing slopes. Many of these can be found in high street shops. The Dyslexia Shop stocks a wide range of equipment.
- Stencils or templates can be given to help with accurate drawing of shapes.
- Experts in the field agree that handwriting skills need to be developed over time. Ott (1997) states that handwriting is a skill that needs to be taught in a structured way and must be practised. Practice should be carried out 'little' and 'often' for constant reinforcement and to prevent the exercise becoming a chore that the student dreads. As in many other aspects of learning, the dyslexic student needs achievable goals. The dyslexic student may not reach the handwriting 'milestones' at the same rate as his peers.
- Take a sympathetic view of a slow speed of writing. Where possible, give shorter written tasks or chunk tasks to prevent the student feeling overwhelmed by the amount of writing expected of him at one time.
- The comments of Professor Fellgett and the experiences of Rachel and others indicate that, despite rigorous practice, difficulties may persist throughout an educational career and into adulthood. It may be necessary for the student to receive support in the form of a note-taker or to be allowed the use of a word processor in the classroom and during examinations. An assessor will ascertain whether the student may qualify for access arrangements during examinations. This judgement may depend on legibility, speed of writing and/or the effect of weaknesses in this area on the content of the work. A timed example of the student's handwritten work may be compared to a timed dictated or word-processed piece on a similar topic. A word of caution: students with severe motor skills problems may find difficulty in using standard keyboards. Larger keyboards or speech recognition software may be more appropriate.

Left-handed students

- When supporting the student, sit on his right side so that work can be clearly seen.
- Do not try to change laterality.
- Use specialist equipment designed for left-handed individuals such as left-handed scissors.
- Older students should experiment with pens that do not smudge. Changing the angle of writing paper can also prevent smudging and allows the student to see what he has written.

Suggested further reading:

Day-to-Day Dyslexia in the Classroom by Joy Pollock and Elisabeth Waller.

How to Manage and Detect Dyslexia by Philomena Ott.

Handwriting: The Way to Teach it by Rosemary Sassoon.

Handwriting Problems in the Secondary School by Rosemary Sassoon.

The Dyspraxia Foundation can provide further advice on accommodating motor skills difficulties.

Meares-Irlen Syndrome

Should there be a concern, either from the parent or teacher, that a student is experiencing visual problems, the initial referral will be to an optometrist who will check for any problems in binocular vision. If the optometrist can find no orthoptic problems of coordination between the eyes then the possibility of Meares-Irlen Syndrome could be considered.

Meares-Irlen Syndrome will not usually be detected during a routine eye examination. 'It is not an optical problem. It is a problem with the brain's ability to process visual information.' (Irlen 2007)

Students who experience visual perceptual difficulties and/or visual stress, have provided the following descriptions of the symptoms:

- Text blurs
- Text moves around on the page
- 'Words wobble'
- Shadowing or doubling of letters
- There are no spaces between words so it is hard to tell where one word ends and the next starts – seehowharditistoreadwithoutgapsinthewords
- Words disappear
- Letters get thinner/thicker
- 'Text "drips" down the page like a melted candle'
- 'Words form a block in the middle of the page'
- Difficulty with tracking
- 'Words get "taller" near the bottom of a computer screen'
- The lines on squared paper/text boxes move around and cause difficulty in concentration
- Shapes move or 'double up' in maths
- 'Busy' patterns/shapes cause discomfort
- The contrast between black print on white paper causes discomfort leading to headaches, tiredness and lack of concentration
- 'My eyes hurt when I read'.

Visiting the Irlen Institute website (www.irlen.com) will give you useful examples of word distortion.

Any of the above can lead to a reduction in the speed and accuracy of reading and, in many cases, a reluctance to read for any length of time.

It is common for students to believe that these difficulties are 'normal' and are experienced by their peers. It is surprising how many adult learners have managed to survive the whole of their statutory education believing that this is the norm. If you suspect that the student may be experiencing difficulties of this nature (see indications below), asking specific questions based on the list above will usually prompt a description of symptoms experienced by the particular student.

Meares-Irlen Syndrome needs to be diagnosed by an appropriately qualified optometrist, but an Intuitive Overlay Assessment, administered by a trained educational psychologist or specialist teacher, can give an indication that there are difficulties in the area of visual perception. The assessor can ascertain which colour of overlay would be most effective for the individual student and will be able to provide appropriate recommendations.

If these recommendations prove effective after a period of use (4–6 weeks is usually recommended), the student's parent may wish to consult an optometrist who specializes in the diagnosis of Meares-Irlen Syndrome. The optometrist will test the student using an intuitive colorimeter which uses up to 7000 tints. A list of optometrists can be found at www.ceriumvistech.co.uk.

While overlays and lenses can alleviate the symptoms to varying degrees, they should not be viewed as a 'cure' for dyslexia. Occasionally, some students have found that the use of overlays and lenses become less effective over time.

For further information, a visit to the 'frequently asked questions' page on the University of Essex website (www.essex.ac.uk/psychology/overlays/faq) is recommended.

How to recognize visual perceptual difficulties

The following behaviours may be indicative of visual perceptual difficulties or visual stress:

- Losing concentration when reading
- Reading slowly
- Reading the end of one word as the beginning of another
- Frequently looking away from the page and/or appearing to 'refocus'
- Rubbing eyes and blinking after a short period of reading
- Regularly complaining of headaches, 'hurting eyes' or tiredness
- 'Wincing' when presented with 'busy' patterns. The student may also physically distance themselves from the page
- Showing signs of discomfort when reading black text on white paper or on shiny paper
- Lack of concentration/signs of discomfort when presented with lined paper, tables or graphs.

Strategies

- If the student has been identified as needing a coloured overlay, photocopy handouts on appropriately coloured paper where possible.
- Try to source coloured file paper, lined or plain, for students to write on. Lines can be photocopied onto plain coloured paper. Coloured exercise books are available from specialist suppliers such as the Dyslexia Shop.
- The student may also benefit if the background colour could be changed when using a computer.

- Students have stated that, when using a whiteboard, it often helps if the teacher uses a blue, red or green marker rather than black to soften the contrast. However, care must be taken that this does not cause difficulty for students who experience colour blindness.
- When using an interactive whiteboard or power-point presentation, change the background colour to suit the student. Problems may arise when more than one student in your class needs differently coloured backgrounds. It is advisable to avoid the harsh contrast of black on white so, in these instances, a cream background will probably suffice.
- Computer software such as ReadAble is available which will change the defaults for background and font colour, font size and style, including websites. This is now available in a portable format which can be used by the student in different classrooms. Suppliers Iansyst (www.dyslexic.com) also provide an advisory service.
- Tinted reading rulers are extremely effective, especially for students who also experience difficulty with tracking.

4 Strategies for reading and spelling

Overview

Frith (1985) identified early literacy development as involving three distinct phases of progression:

Logographic: the student begins to link spoken words with the symbols on the page. Initially this will be in the form of the overall shape of the word with the length of the word and the placement of the ascenders and descenders giving shape to the word. Thus 'bold' and 'gagging' would have very different shapes. The student will then progress to recognition of the 'look' of individual words and begins to construct a sight vocabulary.

Alphabetic: during this stage, the student begins to link the letter with its name and sound. He will recognize that words comprise a set of individual sounds. He realizes that he can use his knowledge of sounds to work out a word on a page and to build words from individual sounds.

Orthographic: the student can now recognize familiar words without having to decode every word he reads. He should also be able to work out unfamiliar words quickly and easily using secure knowledge as clues. For example, a student reading the word 'random' for the first time would be able to recognize the syllables 'ran' and 'dom' as parts of other words that he has read. This is the phase that all of us who are fluent readers will have mastered. Imagine how long it would take to read a 400-page novel if every word had to be decoded.

Consider the skills needed for success in each of these stages; the logographic stage requires sound visual memory and processing skills, the alphabetic stage good phonological processing, auditory memory and processing skills, and the orthographic stage must enlist the efficient use of the central executive area of the working memory (see 'memory' in Chapter 3). It could also be argued that the alphabetic phase may not be secure if the student does not have a good visual memory of the symbols. It is not surprising that the dyslexic student, who may have weaknesses in one or several of these areas, can have difficulty in mastering the basic skills needed for reading and spelling.

As the student progresses to reading sentences, comprehension becomes an issue. The student who finds decoding slow and arduous may get so caught up in the process of decoding the words that he has forgotten what he has read.

The student with secure phonological processing skills may be able to decode words successfully but will not be able to gain meaning from a sentence due to weakness in memory or processing.

Reading ability can, therefore, vary considerably. A 14-year-old dyslexic student may have a far higher single word reading age than his dyslexic classmate as his decoding skills are stronger but processing difficulties may mean that his comprehension skills are comparatively weaker.

Many students develop compensatory skills, often using their strong verbal ability to focus on contextual or semantic clues when reading which makes it difficult for the teacher or parent to recognize the signs of dyslexia. A student who can decode single words confidently may be deemed to be an 'able' reader but he may not be able to understand what he has read.

At my children's primary school, the stalwart group of volunteer 'reading mums' were asked to listen to the students who were identified as the more able readers and to talk about what they had read. This provided an ideal one-to-one opportunity to check the comprehension skills of a group of students for whom no concerns may have been raised. Even if this identified one student in the group who had difficulties with comprehension, it was a worthwhile exercise.

Difficulties with reading will impact on all areas of the curriculum and the dyslexic student may soon find himself being unable to access the information needed to help him progress. Many of my dyslexic students have felt that the quality of their work has been diminished through the inability to carry out independent reading to enhance their knowledge of subjects. One Year 11 student said that he felt that his knowledge of the world was 'narrow' compared to his peers and that he was also unable to extend his personal interests. A Year 7 student became very dispirited as the content of text suitable for his reading ability was rapidly becoming far less challenging and interesting for him intellectually. Both students exhibited signs of a lowering of self-esteem and interest in learning.

Difficulties with spelling can affect the fluency and quality of the student's writing at an early stage; he may 'lose the thread' of what he wants to write and it is common for students to use words that they can spell rather than those which they wish to use.

Suggesting strategies for reading and spelling for the dyslexic student is not a straightforward task. The following strategies do not correspond to age-related reading milestones as the Year 8 student may still be encountering difficulties expected of a Year 3 student in some areas. Instead, I have tried to recount the difficulties in the order in which the students may encounter them.

It must be remembered that most students will have varying levels of strengths and weaknesses and it may be necessary to 'dip in' to suggestions at different levels. Knowledge of the student's learning style and interests will also help the class teacher, support assistant or specialist teacher to devise teaching programmes or strategies for effective reading.

> Remediation is most effective when it is delivered at the student's pace of learning. Palmenti (2000) paraphrased part of the ethos of the Orton-Gillingham approach to reading as 'go as fast as you can but as slow as you need to'.

Regardless of the method or methods of teaching reading employed and the degree of success achieved by other students in the class, the dyslexic student may still find difficulty in learning to read and spell. The teacher may often be frustrated by the fact that her sterling efforts in differentiating materials or employing combinations of reading programmes are having little effect on the student's progress in reading and the decision will be made that specialist teaching is required.

Some schools may employ a specialist teacher who can provide individual tuition for the students and act in an advisory capacity for classroom teachers and learning support assistants. Clusters of schools may be able to tap into the services provided in a specialist unit based in the area. Parents may employ specialist teachers in the home. In any of the situations, it is essential that the work carried out by the specialist teacher is communicated to all involved in the student's learning, including parents and support staff. In this way, learning can be reinforced in the classroom and home. For example, the Year 5 teacher may wish to reinforce work on spelling patterns given in individual lessons delivered by the specialist teacher.

The teacher can record types of reading and spelling errors to help the specialist teacher with the ongoing assessment process. Strategies used by students for reading and spelling can also be noted. Support staff can be trained to carry out this role and some parents may be willing to be involved in this process.

Teaching programmes

In the late 1920s, psychiatrist and neurologist Dr Samuel Orton pioneered the wider use of multisensory teaching of phonics. His later work with Anna Gillingham led to the Orton-Gillingham Approach to reading, writing and spelling. Gillingham subsequently worked with Bessie Stillman (1960) to produce the impressive work *Remedial Training for Children with Specific Disability in Reading, Spelling and*

Penmanship (now known as the Gillingham Manual). In the 1970s Kathleen Hickey and Beve Hornsby developed their own methods based on similar principles. Multi-sensory, cumulative and structured teaching is the basis of most teaching programmes.

There are many programmes that the specialist teacher may use, including the following. It will be helpful if you could investigate which programme the specialist teacher is using in order to prepare support for the student in the classroom.

- *Alpha to Omega* by Beve Hornsby, Frula Shear and Julie Pool. There is now a teacher's handbook and accompanying student's book.
- *The Hickey Multi-Sensory Language Course* by Jean Augur, Suzanne Briggs and Margaret Combley
- *The Bangor Dyslexia Teaching System* by Elaine Miles
- Units of Sound is a computer-based multisensory reading intervention programme which can be used independently by the student with guidance from a teacher or support assistant. Specialist and non-specialist staff can undertake inexpensive distance-learning courses. Details are available from Dyslexia Action.

> **The most commonly used individual reading and spelling programmes will use multisensory, structured, sequential and cumulative methods of teaching. Specialist teaching should not be carried out in isolation; the structure of the programme used by the specialist teacher can be discussed with the classroom teacher to enable her to follow the student's progress and adapt materials to reinforce learning across all subject areas of the curriculum.**

Early reading and spelling skills

It is often difficult for the teacher to find or adapt materials that are suitable for both the student's reading and spelling ability and his chronological age. Knowledge of the student's learning styles and interests can be of great help. A specialist teacher will have built a good library of worksheets, games and other materials that you could borrow for ideas. Most of the suppliers listed in the back of this book will stock worksheets, books and materials to help the dyslexic student with reading and spelling. A favourite range of mine and my students is the Stile dyslexia range of materials. This is a self-checking system using trays with numbered and coloured tiles and books of reading and spelling tasks of all levels. They can be used as practice, for the individual student or as a whole-class exercise, for a variety of programmes.

Reading

- Make alphabet rainbows (see sequencing).
- When teaching the sounds of letters, use flashcards with pictures on one side and letters on the other, using the picture for reinforcement. Take care when making or choosing flashcards as pictures should represent the pure sound of the letter. 'Train' is not a suitable word as it starts with a blend. 'Table' is better. If in doubt, buy flashcards from a specialist supplier. These can be adapted for the older student who may wish to decide which pictures to use (clip art may be needed for more complex words unless you are capable of producing a good image of an iguana). This exercise will also allow the student a degree of ownership of his learning which is essential for the older student.
- Use the techniques to enlist muscle memory to help with handwriting (see 'motor skills' in Chapter 3) to reinforce the shapes of letters. The student can sound the letter as he is producing the shape to link sound and shape.
- Devise games to help with auditory discrimination. I use two 'post boxes' (brightly coloured gift-boxes with a slit cut in each) with the individual sounds to be identified blu-tacked onto each (example 'e' and 'a'). Cards with words containing the sound (for example, 'pen') are read to the student. Without looking at the card, he places it in the appropriate box. This is repeated with differently worded cards. At the end of the 'game', the cards are removed from each box and the student can check the cards with the letters on the box to see if he has posted them correctly. This can be adapted for the older student using appropriate vocabulary.
- Wooden and plastic letters are an excellent multisensory way of allowing the student to experiment with combinations of letters to build words. Partners in Education stock sets of plastic letters comprising blue consonants and red vowels.
- The reading manual 'Toe by Toe' can be used by the teacher, learning support assistant or parent. It needs to be used on a regular basis (20 minutes per day is the recommended maximum). Students have worked on this before the start of school or during registration periods. Parental help can be an invaluable contribution to the success of this programme.
- Help the student to segment words. Tapping on the table helps to count each syllable.
- Older students can segment words in newspapers using a pen to draw vertical lines between each syllable. This can be practised at home (after parents have read the newspaper).
- Picture cards can be sorted into sets of matching initial letters, rhymes or whichever concept the student is working on.
- Give a group of students a rhyme or initial sound. Ask the group to make the funniest/longest sentence. Encourage the group to expand each other's sentences: 'the cat caught the rat and sat on the mat' could become 'the cat caught the rat in a hat and sat on the mat'.
- Word slides and word wheels are quite simple to make. The older student may prefer to make these himself.

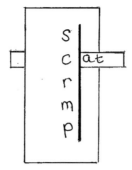

Figure 6 A word slide

- Place coloured stickers at the beginning of lines of texts to ensure that the student with tracking problems starts reading in the correct place.
- Read new text to the student before he reads it, tracking the words with your finger for him to follow.
- The older student who has persistent problems with tracking may need to use a reading ruler (available from Crossbow). Ann Arbor stock an excellent variety of materials, books and worksheets to help with tracking.
- Do not discourage the use of fingers to help with tracking – it may be the student's preferred method.
- Paired reading enables the student to gain enjoyment from reading as he can be given a word when he gets 'stuck', giving his reading experience greater fluency, although it is suggested that prompts such as looking at what the word looks like or using semantic or contextual clues are given before 'jumping in' with the word. There is the opportunity for praise both for correct responses and efforts. Paired reading can be carried out with parents, support staff, the classroom teacher and as part of a 'buddy' system.
- Paired reading also enables the teacher, teaching assistant or parent to note how the student is tackling the task of reading. One teacher gathered parents for a short 'training session' and asked if they could record errors in reading diaries. The information was later relayed to the specialist teacher.
- Students should choose their own reading material for paired reading.
- The student is given models of the pronunciation of words which can be rehearsed later. This can add to the learning experience as definitions can be discussed.
- Use cloze sheets to encourage the early use of contextual clues.
- Do not rush the dyslexic student when he is reading or spelling as this can damage confidence in his ability.
- Enlist the help of parents or learning support assistants to tape text. The student can listen and read at the same time. Information is processed through two channels which allows the student to use his stronger skills while developing weaker ones.

Spelling

- Discuss spelling rules as a whole-class activity. Give the word 'hat': 'What does this say?', 'What does it sound like when we add the magic 'e'?', 'What did we start with?', 'What have we now?' Write the words on the board. A good individual multisensory exercise is to give the student a board and magnetic letters so that the 'e' can be added and taken away several times, the student giving the sound of the words at each change.

- Make pictorial images for letters that are transposed. Try this for the letters 'b' and 'd'. The 'bedposts' must be at the ends of the word.

Figure 7 A pictorial image

- Link words when teaching homophones. 'There' can be linked to 'here' (here and there) to help with their/there confusion. Visualization can be used: you 'hear' with your 'ear'. Pictorial representation is very effective.
- Use colour or embolden letters to highlight spelling rules. Pu**tt**ing rules clearly can help.
- Avoid giving spelling lists containing more then one spelling pattern as this will prove confusing if he has to switch between patterns.
- The dyslexic student is unlikely be able to learn spellings by rote, and will not learn by being forced to correct spellings by copying them endlessly.
- Many teachers are confounded by the ease with which the dyslexic student will be able to understand and apply spelling rules during one lesson and the equal ease he will show in his ability to forget these by the next lesson.
- The last three points highlight the need for a structured programme delivered at the student's pace of learning.
- The 'Look, Say, Cover, Say, Write and Check' system of teaching spelling has been proven to be successful for many students as it is a multisensory exercise involving auditory (say), visual (look and check) and kinaesthetic (write) input. The sequence goes:
  - Look at the word. Notice familiar and unusual spelling patterns
  - Say the word, matching the sounds with the letters or syllables
  - Cover the word
  - Say the word again. Visualize the word as you are saying it
  - Write the word
  - Check to see if the spelling is correct.
- Some teachers use Look, Cover, Write and Check (omitting the phonetic link). Critics of this method point out that this is a visual and motor exercise which will not be suitable for a student with weak visual processing or visual sequential memory skills.
- Research has shown that the spellings of words written in a cursive script are much more likely to be retained.

Higher level reading and spelling skills

Reading

- Differentiating text does not simply mean rewriting worksheets in 'simpler' language or précising text. Differentiation should involve presenting material 'differently' in a manner or medium that the student can access. This may involve using more accessible or less text but it can also involve the use of pictures, flow charts, highlighting key words, changing size or style of fonts or giving definitions of subject-specific words at the bottom of the page. The student could also be allowed to complete the sheet in various ways; completing cloze sentences, using illustrations, giving verbal responses to questions or word-processing answers.

- Skimming and scanning skills are extremely valuable tools for the dyslexic student. The terms 'skimming' and 'scanning' are often thought to be interchangeable but are two separate skills, albeit ones that are often carried out in tandem.

  Skimming involves reading the text quickly to get a gist of a paragraph. When reading significant amounts of text, the topic of a paragraph can usually be ascertained by reading the first and last sentences.

  Scanning involves reading the text quickly to identify key words.

  Practice may be needed to use these skills effectively but this can be done as a whole-class exercise which will be beneficial to all students.

  Skimming and scanning give the student an overview of the topic which helps the student with slow reading or poor comprehension skills to keep on track.

- The dyslexic student may find that highlighting key words may be helpful for note-taking or revision. Transparent highlighter tape (available from the Dyslexia Shop) can be used for books belonging to the school or library. One student used two colours when highlighting words; one colour for words that he needed for revision and another for words that he could not spell but which he believed he would need to use in an exam or essay. He later transferred the 'spelling' words into a personal spelling dictionary.

- Students with poor memory or processing skills should 'chunk' text into manageable pieces and take frequent, short breaks when reading. Research into memory indicates that learning is most effective when it is chunked into short periods with rest breaks. This is particularly pertinent to individuals with memory or processing problems as the brain can easily become 'overloaded' when given too much information. The consequence of this is that much of the information will then be lost or incorrectly remembered.

- Students should take regular notes from text for revision or essay writing as short-term memory or processing problems may mean that they will forget crucial facts if attempting to remember the content of large amounts of text.

  - Many dyslexic students will automatically use contextual and/or semantic clues but others may need support to develop this skill. Cloze sheets can be used to fill in missing words, ideas or concepts.
  - Encourage the student to use mental images from the text to help with understanding. If this proves difficult, read the book to the student or the whole class and ask them to close their eyes to imagine how it looks. This will also help him to remember the plot of a book.
  - Use pictures or diagrams when creating worksheets. Try to access illustrated textbooks. The student will use the visual trigger to remember the worded information.
  - Before starting to read a set text which the student will perceive as difficult (any of the works of Shakespeare, for example) investigate suitable online revision sites or books. The student can read

a précis of the plot or individual chapter which will help with comprehension of the complete text. Videos and DVDs give a visual representation of 'difficult' text.

- There is a wide range of reading material now available in CD format or downloadable from the internet including many set texts for GCSE English. SmartPass student audio guides are available on CD and MP3 (the Learning Shop stock a range) and include commentary and analysis written by teachers. Many older dyslexic students find that the multisensory activity of simultaneously listening to and reading a book helps understanding, memory and retention of information. Students have commented that this is even more effective if it has been the normal way of working since primary school. Where textbooks in other subject areas are not available, parents or learning support assistants could be enlisted to record text.
- Audio recording also enables the student to work independently.

- If text is to be studied in the classroom and the dyslexic student has not had the opportunity to scan the text beforehand, write key themes, unfamiliar or subject-specific words on the board.
- Give the students questions on the text before reading. This will help focus on key points. Whole-class discussion and prediction of text can also act as a focus.
- It may help if students are given text/handouts prior to a lesson in order that they may read them beforehand to gain meaning.
- Check if the student is comfortable with reading aloud. They can participate orally in other ways – answering questions, role play, giving verbal demonstrations to their peer group.
- Ensure that the student has sufficient time to read text in class.
- The student may need someone to read for him in class. If no support is available, a buddy system could be set in place.
- Check that understanding has taken place.
  - If the reading level of a set textbook is above that of the student's reading ability, try to source materials around the subject that the student will be able to read.
  - Encourage the student to use prior knowledge of a subject to help extend his interest in further reading. The student may automatically label a new book as 'too hard' or 'too long'. Skim the book with the student and pick out topics which he has studied, shown an interest in or has some knowledge of (he may be an avid watcher of television wildlife or history programmes or has a pertinent hobby). Prior knowledge will enable him to use contextual clues more easily. The student, who is likely to perceive the book as being potentially enjoyable and useful, will have gained a sense of achievement at being able to read a 'hard' book. If possible, enlist the help of a learning support assistant or parent as this could involve a significant amount of paired reading.
- If the student is showing signs of a lack of self-esteem in his reading ability or is losing interest in reading, refer to a recent success, no matter how small the step may have been. The student may have finished a difficult passage or used his reading to talk about the topic in class. The student who lacks self-esteem will often look at the amount that he has been unable to read and may need to be reminded of his achievements.
- If the student is constructing a personal dictionary, ensure that he is using it for reading (reinforcement of unfamiliar words) as well as spelling.
- All subject teachers should keep a dictionary readily available for use by all students in the classroom. The dyslexic student may be reluctant to use his own dictionary if he is the only student doing so. A good psychological tactic is for the teacher to be seen to refer to a dictionary herself as this makes it an 'acceptable' activity.

Spelling

- There is a tendency for the dyslexic student to resort to illegible writing in an attempt to cover up spelling errors. Point out that the teacher may be able to interpret an inaccurate spelling but cannot do this if she is unable to read it. Emphasize the importance of this in examinations where there is the potential to lose marks.
- The dyslexic student may panic or get lost when attempting to spell longer words. It is common for the first syllable to be correctly spelt before the student becomes confused or gives up. Encourage him to take a calm, systematic approach. Use existing secure knowledge of rules to build up syllable by syllable, sounding each before writing. Students with stronger visual skills may prefer to picture the syllable, possibly in the context of a known word. Try using 'hippopotamus' as an example; each syllable uses early spelling rules but the student is usually very impressed with the result. This can highlight areas for revision; one student used this technique and arrived at 'accompaknee' (accompany) and I regularly see 'occupie' as given spelling during the WRAT4 assessment.
- This also prevents loss or repetition of syllables ('opptunty' for opportunity or 'remememeber' for remember).
- The student with very weak phonological skills will still find extreme difficulty in building words phonetically. If the student is undertaking a spelling programme, check his progress to ensure that you do not have an unrealistic expectation of his working knowledge of spelling patterns.
- Encourage the student with stronger visual skills to write a word to see if it 'looks right' then check the spelling with the dictionary.
- Subject-specific spellings, particularly scientific ones, can be built up from a core word. The student attempting to spell polycarbonate can extract the word carbon which he will have met before and add the prefix and suffix.
- The student may need to use a computer with spell-check and grammar check facilities when writing extended pieces.
- As mentioned in the reading section above, encourage all students to use dictionaries in class. Hand-held spell-checkers can be used.
- It is a common complaint from dyslexic students that they are told to use a dictionary but do not have the secure phonological skills to do so. A student spent a considerable amount of time looking through 'des.' and 'dec.' words to find 'disease'. Some dyslexic students find the ACE (Aurally Coded English) dictionary helpful. The dictionary has an aural coding system enabling the student to find the word by how it sounds.
- Similarly, the student cannot easily access a dictionary due to poor sequencing skills. He may find it helpful to write down the alphabet and stick it in the front of his dictionary.
- Students can construct their own 'dictionaries'. Subject-specific words which they will regularly encounter or words that they regularly mis-spell can be entered for ease of reference and to be used for rehearsal of spelling.
- Continue to link words when students continue to confuse homophones. Encourage the older student to devise his own links.
- Mnemonics aid memory using sounds or imagery as prompts. The use of mnemonics is often used in spelling, a common one being for the word **B**ig **E**lephants **C**an't **A**lways **U**se **S**mall **E**xits (there are several variations of this). Encourage the student to make up his own as this aids memory. Be aware that the student may not be able to spell the words that you have given in the mnemonic.
- Use pictures to reinforce the image.

Case study

Lizzie, a mature student, became quite agitated when the subject arose as she had a long-standing 'hatred' of mnemonics. Her Year 6 teacher had insisted that all students remember the above mnemonic for 'because'. Lizzie consistently spelt this 'becouse' and was frequently told off by the teacher. Had the teacher asked her why she made this mistake she would have discovered that Lizzie spelt the word 'always' as 'orlways'.

- Comments about poor spellings are unhelpful and unnecessary – the student will be only too aware of his difficulties.
- It would be helpful if the content of any written work is considered above the way work is written. It is easy initially to misjudge the quality of the content of a piece of written work if spelling is poor, especially at the beginning of the teacher/student relationship when the teacher may not be aware of the student's strengths.
- If spelling is so weak that work is illegible, it may be necessary for support to be put in place in the classroom to help with recording work and note-taking. It may be necessary to raise concerns with the SENCO as access to examination arrangements may be needed.

Suggested further reading for reading and spelling:

Dyslexia: A Teenager's Guide by Dr Sylvia Moody.

Help Students Improve Their Study Skills. A Handbook for Teaching Assistants in Secondary Schools by Jane Dupree.

'Supporting dyslexic pupils 7-14 across the curriculum' by Sally Raymond. (A selection of excellent photocopiable worksheets).

Day-to-Day Dyslexia in the Classroom by Joy Pollock and Elisabeth Waller.

Dyslexia (2nd edition) by Gavin Reid.

How to Manage and Detect Dyslexia by Philomena Ott.

Toe by Toe by Keda Cowling and Harry Cowling.

Alpha to Omega Teachers Handbook. The A–Z of teaching reading, writing and spelling by Beve Hornsby, Frula Shear and Julie Pool. This programme should be delivered by a specialist teacher, but I believe that it is of interest for the non-specialist teacher to gain understanding into the structure of the teaching.

The Gift of Dyslexia: Why Some of the Brightest People Can't Read and How They Can Learn (2nd revised edition) by Ronald Davis.

Choosing appropriate text

For a student to gain success and enjoyment from reading, the following must be considered:

- Does the subject of the book, newspaper article, webpage interest the student?
- Is he motivated to read it?
- Is he comfortable with the font, size of print, colour of the page?
- Does the complexity of the vocabulary and sentence match his reading ability?
- What will he gain from reading the book (enjoyment, knowledge)?
- Does the book contain too much information in too short a time?

The dyslexic student may have become a reluctant reader due to his inability to read given material, regularly 'losing the plot' of books or being given text that is compatible with his reading age but whose content is 'babyish'. It can, therefore, be important to ensure that reading material fits as many of the criteria above to promote an interest in reading. The debate as to the value of reading comics and magazines is likely to continue but the look of satisfaction on the face of the dyslexic student who has managed to get to the end of *any* piece of written material and gained enjoyment from it is a joy to behold.

Case study

At the age of 15, Adam proudly confided that he had just finished reading the first book in the 'Harry Potter' series; this was the only book that he had managed to read from cover to cover. At just over 200 pages, this is a considerable feat for a student who had not been able to complete shorter books that his teachers and parents had thought to be within his capabilities. It transpired that there were several motivating factors behind this achievement: he quickly became engaged in the story, he was desperate to join in his friends' discussions about the book and he had seen the film so knew the plot, which prevented him getting lost. Adam announced that he was now eager to start reading work by other authors. Adam's single word reading and comprehension scores were at the lower end of the average range for his age but his well below average speed of reading had previously meant that he had found reading to be a laborious task.

The online bookseller, Amazon, states that the reading age of this book is 9–12. The research of Klare (1963) found that most students prefer to read below their reading level and it has been suggested that reading material should be as much as 2 years below the student's reading level to ensure full comprehension and fluency when reading. It would appear that the book fulfilled the fourth criterion for success.

Reading age tests

Reading age tests involve calculations based on the length of sentences and the number of syllables in the words. The two most commonly used are the Flesch-Kincaid test and the Gunning 'FOG' Readability Test. The FOG test is usually regarded as more suitable for the upper end of Key Stage 2 and secondary level.

Flesch-Kincaid Formula

Reading age $= (0.39 \times \text{ASL}) + (11.8 \times \text{ASW}) - 10.59$

ASL = average sentence length (number of words divided by number of sentences).

ASW = average number of syllables per word (total number of syllables divided by the number of words).

Gunning 'FOG' Readability Test

Take 3 samples of 100 words each.

Find L, the average sentence length (number of words divided by number of sentences). Estimate the number of sentences to the nearest tenth.

Find N. Count the number of words in each sample with more than 3 syllables and calculate the average.

Reading age $= [(\text{L} + \text{N}) \times 0.4] + 5$ years.

An easy method to check the readability of text found on the computer (for example when compiling worksheets or using information from the internet) is through the toolbar on Microsoft Word:

1. Go to tools, click Options, and then click on Spelling & Grammar.
2. Select the Check Grammar with spelling check box.
3. Select the Show Readability statistics check box, and then click OK.
4. Click Spelling and Grammar on the Standard toolbar.

Word will display the reading level of the document after it has finished checking spelling and grammar. To skip this process, press 'ignore all'.

The greatest difficulty is in finding material for the older student that suits both his interest and reading ability. Some texts may have unexpected reading levels; *Lord of the Flies*, which often appears as a set text for GCSE, has a reading age of 11 years. It is worth carrying out a reading age check on text that is deemed to be of potential interest to a student.

There are at least two specialist publishers of fiction published specifically for dyslexic students:

Barrington Stoke publishes books that use vocabulary and sentence structures appropriate for reading ages 8 and above but whose content appeals to the older student. The books are graded in interest age ranges, are printed on off-white paper and have a modified font.

New Leaf publish material written for the older teenager and adult (some have adult content). The books are ideal for the student with significant reading difficulty as they are very short. Companion CDs of recorded text are available for many of the titles. All of the titles are written by dyslexic adults and are chosen for publication by focus groups made up of dyslexic readers. The idea of books being written by dyslexic individuals for other dyslexic readers can be motivational for the student who is lacking in self-esteem.

5   Study Skills

Overview

My work with dyslexic students in the post-compulsory sector and with individuals in employment has highlighted the importance of the development of effective study skills on success in lifelong learning and in the workplace. Students in colleges, universities and in vocational training who have developed successful strategies for study during their school careers can often develop these further to cope with the higher level skills needed in further or higher education. There is a marked difference in the level of difficulty encountered with transference to a higher level of learning between those students who have been implementing successful strategies and those who are 'starting from scratch'.

Many have been able to adapt strategies for the workplace. Employers are impressed by the individual's ability to outline his methods of accommodating weaknesses and discuss how these could be implemented in the particular working environment.

Weak processing, sequencing, memory and organization skills may become increasingly evident as the student meets higher level study skills, whether it be at Key Stages 3 or 4 or during a post-compulsory education career. Indeed, dyslexia may not have been considered until the student encounters difficulties in this area. It must be emphasized again that signs of dyslexia may manifest themselves at any age and difficulties with, for example, revision, planning, organization and note-taking may all be indicators that the student is dyslexic. If there are concerns, these should be noted and discussed with the SENCO.

As with reading and spelling, the dyslexic student may need support to develop effective study skills. Depending on the resources and available manpower in the school, it may be possible for the student to spend time on a one-on-one basis with a specialist teacher or learning support assistant. This often allows the student and teacher the time to explore fully the student's thinking and learning styles and the way he approaches tasks as well as giving the opportunity to practise the skills on current work. Support in the classroom is an invaluable way of tackling difficulties as they arise.

Note-taking

When considering the best strategies to help a student with note-taking, it is advisable to consider the purpose of the note-taking exercise. It may be deemed important that the student is supported to develop strategies to take his own notes from the board or from speech to prepare him for independent learning in further or higher education or in the workplace. The purpose may be to encourage all students to sort or augment relevant information.

Despite receiving the same instructions as his peers, some dyslexic students, due to slow processing speeds, weak working memory or slow or illegible handwriting may find this an impossible task. The student will often attempt to take notes which will prove unintelligible later. In the process of this attempt, he will not have been able to follow the gist of the lesson. In effect, he may have missed a substantial part or all of a lesson. The quality of note-taking can influence the quality of a written piece and the effectiveness of revision, areas in which the dyslexic student may encounter other difficulties.

The student may need support to develop and practise the following strategies:

Note-taking from speech

- Help the student to practise sorting information to enable him to record notes in bullet point form. Where available, a learning support assistant could take on this role. This could also be carried out as a whole-class exercise.
- Where it is not detrimental to your teaching and the learning of other students adapt the pace of delivery to allow the student time to make notes.
- The older student may wish to use a dictaphone to record lessons although some specialist teachers and students feel that background noise can be too disruptive when the recording is played back. He can make his own notes at his own pace later.
- It may help if the student is given a mind map template, cloze sheets for him to record single word notes or a sheet comprising key points of topics (with the intention that he adds to these notes).
- The student could be given an outline of the key points of the lesson or details of pages of a textbook containing relevant information beforehand. He can then read these in advance to gain the gist of the lesson. This requires an efficient communication system involving establishing pick-up points and times and the student developing a habit of checking for notes.
- Ensure that the student has written sufficient information to enable him to complete homework and has accurately recorded information and instructions for homework.

- A decision may have to be made that the student will have to be provided with notes and that he will use his energies in concentrating on the delivery of the lesson (which may already prove difficult if he has a slow speed of auditory processing).

Note-taking from the board

- Ensure that the student has sufficient time to write down all information.
- Ensure that information is written down correctly.
- Use different colours on the whiteboard to make the text easier to follow and understand. This may not be appropriate if another student is colour blind.
- Key words can be highlighted in different colours to help with bullet-pointing notes.
- It may be necessary to provide a note-taker as other students' learning must be considered.
- If so, it is preferable if the student has some input into the process by indicating which information he wishes to be recorded otherwise there is a tendency towards passive learning.
- A 'study buddy' system can be used for the above, especially during lessons where lengthy note-taking is unavoidable. The student could be paired with a 'study buddy' who has weaknesses in areas that the dyslexic student has strengths. In this way, the dyslexic student feels part of a partnership rather than 'taking' from the other student all the time.

Note-taking from text

- Notes should be taken frequently to avoid forgetting or inaccurately remembering information.
- Notes can be bullet-pointed using key words or phrases.
- If a student is compiling a personal dictionary comprising subject-specific vocabulary and words that he may mis-spell, he should keep this to hand so that words can be included immediately.
- Pictorial notes can be made.
- The student can use mind maps.
- Colour-code notes using differently coloured pens or highlighting words.

Case study

Louise, a Year 12 student, used a large notebook that she used for taking notes from text and during lessons. The notes were written in a variety of colours. Louise explained that she was a sequential thinker and did not like mind maps but had adapted the idea of using colour into her notes. Before she started reading, she made a basic plan of the content of her paragraphs and allocated a colour to each. When reading, she made notes in the appropriate colour. She was able to find relevant information for each paragraph when planning and writing work. Louise had a ballpoint pen containing different coloured refills which she constantly changed when taking notes in class. Impressively, she was able to use this technique at high speed, although none of her peers would sit next to her due to the constant clicking of the pen as she changed colour.

Strategies for note-taking must always be implemented with the student's strengths and weaknesses in mind. The key factors are that he must be in possession of notes that contain all the information needed for writing or revision in a format that he can access.

Revision

Revision can be a very stressful exercise for dyslexic students who may feel overloaded with information. The student who is also worried about reading questions, spelling and planning answers may feel extremely pressurized. If the student feels that his revision has been effective, this can give him greater confidence in tackling exams and relieve stress.

Strategies

- Mind maps can be a very effective tool for revision but these do not suit all students' learning styles.
- The student can use record cards for many subject areas and types of revision. He may wish to write a subject-specific word or formula on one side of the card and a definition on the other or set himself questions on one side and answers on the other.
- Note-taking from text books should contain essential information to reduce the amount of reading and the need for the brain to process unnecessary information.
- It is a common occurrence for dyslexic students to believe that they have to revise more intensely. Murdoch (1962) found that items heard first in a list (primacy) and items heard last in a list (recency) were more likely to be remembered than those in the middle of a list. This work has been extended by many others and the conclusion has been reached that more information is retained during shorter periods of memorizing information. Studies suggest that an individual should study for a period of 25 to 50 minutes before taking a 10 minute break which ideally should involve some creative or physical activity. The students can take some ownership of his studies by learning to realize/be aware when his brain is becoming overloaded (or, as one student described it 'fried').
- The student should construct a revision timetable that is realistic and builds in time for relaxation. There may be parental pressure on the student to revise more intensely. The student may need your support to explain to his parents that his timetable will be more effective for him.
- Constant reviewing is essential for revision. Ebbinghaus (1913) described the exponential nature of forgetting. This was subsequently plotted as a graph and became known as the 'forgetting curve'. Continuing research shows that information regularly needs to be reviewed if it is to be retained.
- Where possible the student should revise from his own notes as he is more likely to remember vocabulary and phrases that he uses.
- Use strategies for memory that are familiar and appeal to his learning style; the visual learner could use pictures, mnemonics and visualize facts, events or storylines (particularly good for history and English). He may wish to picture himself carrying out a science experiment.
- If the student has a weak visual memory and strong auditory memory, find a willing volunteer to record revision notes (enlist the help of parents or support staff).
- Help the student to organize materials into a logical order of revision.

- Using a dictaphone, the student can record his own notes and replay them as often as necessary to reduce the amount of reading required.
- A popular teacher, Mike, constantly reminds all of his students to RTFQ (read the flipping question) shortly before the exams as many, often through exam nerves, will often not read the question carefully and will include unnecessary information or, in worst cases, write a completely irrelevant answer. The dyslexic student with weaker decoding or comprehension skills will find it beneficial to work through past papers to familiarize himself with the style of question and language used (including instructional words such as 'discuss, explain, give examples of, estimate').

> Revision should be ordered and chunked and regular breaks taken to avoid memory overload. Frequent review of information is essential.

Planning and structuring work

A teacher recently commented that she spent a great deal time teaching her Year 10 and 11 students the facts that they needed to know and effective ways of remembering them but had not given them the tools to convey effectively this knowledge in their written work. We agreed that planning should be introduced from Key Stage 2. The dyslexic student whose difficulties with processing, sequencing or organization will give rise to difficulties with planning will find this a greater obstacle if he is trying to develop this skill at a stage in his school career when he is also facing an increasing amount and complexity of information to process and remember.

The 'Six Box Trick'

My thanks go to Steve Thomas for showing me the 'Six Box Trick' (Figure 8) which was effective when used as a whole-class exercise for a group of Year 5 and 6 students. The 'Six Box Trick' has subsequently proved to be particularly beneficial to students of all ages who cannot structure their written stories.

The student writes his initial ideas in the relevant boxes. As he expands his story, he can write further details in each or any of the boxes. The order of events can be numbered to help sequence the events.

WHO?	WHERE?	WHEN?
Sam and James - rescue Ed and Harry - got stuck	Sam and James on the way home from the moon - 2 In deepest space - 1 Collecting moon rock - 2	2020
WHAT IS HAPPENING?	**WHAT HAPPENS NEXT?**	**HOW DOES IT END?**
Ed and Harry's spaceship broken down	Sam and James rescue Ed and Harry Spaceship towed home Ed and Harry scared	They all get home safely

Figure 8 The 'Six Box Trick'

Case study

Ben wrote this story: 'Sam and James were on their way back from the moon and they had to rescue the spaceship that had engine trouble but they all got back safely. They towed the spaceship. The men in the other spaceship were called Ed and Harry. This all happened in the future. They were all very frightened.' With the use of the 'Six Box Trick' the story became: 'In the Year 2020, Sam and James were in deepest outer space on their way back from the moon where they had been collecting moon rock. They got a distress call from Ed and Harry whose spaceship had engine trouble. Sam and James rescued Ed and Harry and towed their ship through space. Ed and Harry were very frightened but they all got back to Earth safely.'

Spidergrams

Spidergrams and mind maps are often confused. Mind maps (see section on mind mapping) have a more complex structure, although I have seen spidergrams used as a 'blueprint' for a complex mind map. Some students prefer to use spidergrams as an initial method of planning to give them a clear 'picture' of the overall structure of the work or as an initial plan for sequentially written notes. The 'legs' are often numbered in the order in which the information will appear.

An FE student who had used this technique regularly in school was able to extend this idea when planning lengthy assignments and essays by including the number of words that she felt she should use for each topic.

Flow charts and time lines

Sequential thinkers may prefer to plan in a linear fashion. These can use words or pictures or a combination of both.

Students have commented that, when constructing flow charts and time lines by hand, it is sometimes difficult to add in ideas in the middle of a line or chart as the information may become cramped. This can be solved by using a computer to build the line or chart.

Digital recorders/dictaphones

Many older dyslexic students will complain that the most frustrating aspect of dyslexia is the inability to write as fast as they think. Consequently, they may lose ideas or spelling, and sentence structure and handwriting is sacrificed. The student can record his ideas on a dictaphone and replay these at his own pace later. This will allow him to concentrate on the mechanics of writing, secure in the knowledge that his ideas are securely recorded.

Model answers

Discuss titles of essays or answers to questions in the classroom. This may help the dyslexic student to plan his work using an accepted model.

Building and streamlining

Techniques such as those outlined above are most often used to help the student to sort information while he is building a piece of work. Those supporting the student in the classroom or during one-on-one or small group support lessons can discuss the progress of planning and help the student to think how he could expand ideas or include other relevant information. However, these techniques can be used to streamline ideas.

Case study

Emily, a Year 10 student, was dyslexic but her assessment recorded underlying ability levels in the 'upper extreme' range. She had a well-developed intellectual curiosity and often, according to her mother, spent hours in further investigating a topic of study. Emily found planning a task difficult and could not organize her thoughts onto paper. Consequently, when answering a question or writing on a specific aspect of a topic, she tended to write everything she knew about that topic. She lost marks in school examinations as she did not have time to answer all of the questions on a paper and could not give precise answers to the questions. Her essays were often written in 'stream of consciousness' style and often contained irrelevant facts. Emily was asked to construct a spidergram or mind map to help her plan a piece of work with a specific title. She rapidly filled an A3 sheet of paper with her ideas. Her learning support assistant then looked at the title of the essay with her and they systematically crossed out all of the facts on the spidergram that were not relevant to the title. Emily could then start to plan her essay using the pared down information.

Mind Mapping

In 1974, Tony Buzan introduced the technique of Mind Mapping® in his book 'Use Your Head'. By the year 2000, it was estimated that there were over 250 million 'Mind Mappers' worldwide (source: Buzan & Buzan, *The Mind Map Book*). The technique is now regularly being employed by classroom and specialist teachers and support staff to help with planning, revision and note-taking. Some readers of this book will have doubtlessly found other innovative uses for mind maps.

The reactions of students fall into three categories with regards to attitudes toward the use of mind maps; 'they have really helped in many areas of my studies', 'I can't work with them at all' and 'I use them because I've been told to but they seem to be a lot of work for little benefit'. It is the last comment that causes me concern as this situation has arisen for various reasons; one student commented that her teacher was an avid fan of mind maps so everyone had to use them, another was told that all dyslexic students benefit from using mind maps and the third felt under pressure to 'keep up' with her peers who were all successfully using mind maps in the classroom. The teacher of the third student who was using mind mapping as a teaching strategy in history lessons reported that the class, in general, had enthusiastically embraced the idea resulting in an increase in the levels of motivation for study, quality of written work and examination results. As the third student had produced impressive mind maps, the teacher had not realized that this technique did not suit the student's way of working. However, for many dyslexic students, mind mapping has allowed them to use their strengths and has opened the door to an effective method of study.

Mind mapping involves the whole brain as facts need to be analysed before being included in a holistic representation of a topic. However, mind maps often appeal to the right-brained student, the left-brained student preferring to record ideas and information in a linear fashion.

As teachers are now developing the use of mind maps from Key Stage 2 onwards, I presume that most readers of this book will be familiar with the technique. Dupree (2005) suggests that mind mapping skills are taught early on in Key Stage 3. However, for those new to this concept, Figure 9 is an example produced by a Year 7 student, Kate, as an aid to planning an autobiographical essay at the beginning of the year. (Kate is now in Year 10 and redrew this for me as she wanted to change a few personal details.)

The student begins with the central 'trunk' representing the theme of the topic ('About me'). The four 'branches' radiating from the trunk represent the subject of each of her paragraphs. She has then expanded her ideas by adding stems to the branches.

This mind map demonstrates how this student used her strengths and weaknesses to make this technique work for her. She had previously encountered difficulty in planning and structuring her work. Her mind map contains a numbering system which was added when she felt that she had recorded all of the facts and ideas that she wished to include in her essay. This gave her a clear structure to work from. She was a confident speller and used a greater proportion of words to pictures. She commented that she 'drew pictures to help her concentrate when she couldn't think

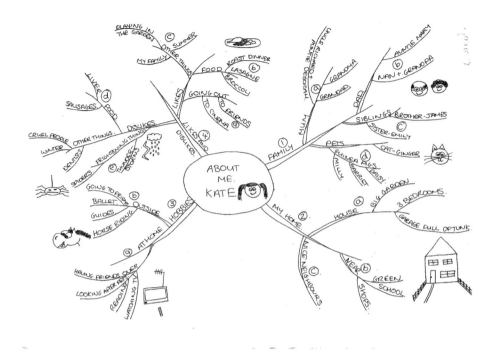

Figure 9 Kate's mind map – About me

of the next idea'. She admitted that she usually gave up when she ran out of ideas but having the map in front of her was a constant reminder of how much work she had done so far; a motivational factor to continue.

The branches of the map are usually drawn in different colours. When the map is being used for revision, this helps the student to chunk the information as he can visualize smaller sections of the map. Buzan (2000) suggests that that all words on the mind map should be printed. The defined shape of the printed letter makes it easier for the mind to 'picture' it. As the physical act of printing text is slower and requires more effort than using a cursive script, it becomes a more memorable exercise and also encourages brevity. Pictures and symbols will help with visualization. Pictures, symbols and key words should be generated by the student to enable him to use these as effective memory triggers. It does not matter how 'silly' or simply drawn pictures are or how obscure key words may appear to others. A mind map must be viewed as a personal working document. The classroom situation, in which a spirit of competition develops when the students 'judge' the quality of pictures or the complexity of the mind map, should be discouraged.

Mind maps are also an effective method of note-taking. When introducing this technique, teachers may give students an outline of a map on which she has written the topic in the stem and the main subheadings in the branches. This is an excellent introduction to the technique but the student should be encouraged to develop this skill independently as part of the process of sorting information

Mind mapping software such as Inspiration and MindGenius (available from Iansyst) is growing in use. This can be ideal for the student who is likely to lose a written map as it can be stored on the computer. The student who prefers information presented in a visual form but dislikes drawing can use clip art. Conversely, the student who enjoys the kinaesthetic experience of drawing may not find this such a rewarding exercise.

Advantages of a mind map

- Acts as an active learning tool which gives students ownership of their learning.
- The student can represent ideas pictorially or in very few words enabling him to record his ideas when planning and access information when revising without the involvement of a large amount of reading.
- All information needed for planning or revising is on one sheet which can be a great help to those students with organizational problems.
- The map can be used as a working document for longer essays or assignments. The student can add information at his own pace. Some dyslexic students have commented that, as they can record information more quickly, this 'grows' more rapidly than a set of sequentially ordered written notes. This helps with self-esteem and motivation.
- Colour and pictures act as visual triggers when revising.
- Many students find mind mapping a fun activity.
- One document can have a dual purpose; the map produced as a planning exercise can be used later for revision.
- The act of constructing the mind map also acts as reinforcement of information.
- Mind maps can be generated/constructed on a computer using specialist software.

Disadvantages

- Mind mapping may not suit all learning styles. A student who is very 'left-brained' may prefer to plan and revise using sequential recording. Study for this student may become less enjoyable and less effective if the use of mind maps is expected of all members of the class.
- Some students find mind maps visually confusing.
- While it may be an advantage to have all information on one sheet, the student could lose all of his work if this sheet gets lost.
- Mind maps are usually produced on A3 (or larger) paper which is not as easy to store or file.
- Mind maps can be time consuming. The student with time management difficulties may not appreciate that he has spent an inordinate amount of time drawing one picture. Others may use this as a 'delaying tactic'. It is difficult for the teacher to ask the student to stop spending too much time on a drawing when the student has been told that this is an acceptable way of working.
- The student may feel that his map is not of the same standard as his peers or may not be happy with the presentation. He must be assured that it is his work and that, if it serves a purpose for him, it is successful.

- Ensure that the student understands the rationale behind the concept of mind mapping to ensure that this is used effectively.

Case study

> Kirsty produced a beautifully constructed mind map that contained pictorial representations and was clearly set out, using colour appropriately. It was noticed that Kirsty did not attempt to use her mind map for revision. When asked why, she replied that she couldn't find the information that she wanted to use and could not remember all of the information on the map when revising as it was 'too busy'. She had not recognized that she could use the colours to help her chunk the information.

> **Ensure that the use of a mind map is appropriate for the individual student's learning style, strengths and weaknesses. A mind map is a personal working document that the student uses actively as a tool for effective revision, planning or note-taking.**

Suggested further reading for study skills:

The Mind Map Book by Tony & Barry Buzan.

Mind Maps for Kids: An Introduction. The Shortcut to Success at School by Tony Buzan.

Mind Maps for Kids; Max Your Memory and Concentration by Tony Buzan.

Help Students Improve Their Study Skills. A Handbook for Teaching Assistants in Secondary Schools by Jane Dupree.

Dyslexia: A Teenager's Guide by Dr Sylvia Moody.

ICT

ICT, whether in the form of computers, audio-visual equipment (including filming, sound recording and photographic equipment) and myriad other forms of technology, is now commonplace within home, educational and social settings. In some cases, the student's confident use of ICT is ahead of the teacher's working knowledge. It is a medium which many students feel comfortable with and enjoy using. Multisensory aspects of ICT can be used as an effective aid to learning for many dyslexic students and the 'fun' aspect can be motivational for many reluctant learners.

Advantages of the use of ICT

- Using a computer with the spell-check facility activated allows the student with poor spelling and/or handwriting to concentrate on the content of his work.
- The dyslexic student may find it easier to draft and edit work. Ideas can be typed, cut and pasted much more quickly by some students whose speed of writing is slow.
- Many students now have access to a computer at home or in school. Consequently, typing skills are developed at an early age.
- The use of ICT is often thought to be something of an insular exercise. The Primary Framework for Literacy and Mathematics suggests whole-class activities involving the use of ICT including phonics photos (words that share the same initial phoneme are recorded on a digital camera), storyboarding using photographs and email stories (a story is developed between two classes in different schools by email). As with any group activity, the dyslexic student can be encouraged to use his strengths to become an active and valued member of the group.
- A dyslexic student who receives a high level of support may like the opportunity to work independently. This can be carried out effectively if the work is adapted to the student's level and style of working or if specialist software is being used.
- Students can transfer work onto disc or memory stick to complete at home. It may be possible to ask parents to purchase appropriate software so that the student can reinforce skills at home.
- The presentation of work can be improved. Work written in poor handwriting littered with spelling errors does little for the student's self-esteem. One Year 6 student changed the font of work that was to be displayed to one that resembled handwriting in order that it did not 'stick out' from the handwritten efforts of his classmates. It was pointed out to him that this was unnecessary as a different mode of presentation should be seen as a positive feature of his work but he had not yet developed the confidence to show his peers that he thought and worked in a different way.
- Effective use of technology can enable the student to differentiate tasks and allow him a degree of ownership in his learning.
- The Primary Framework for Literacy and Mathematics suggests that students can use software to create crosswords for their peers to solve. Crossword puzzles may be difficult to solve for the dyslexic student who has difficulty with spelling. However, word searches are a good alternative; the dyslexic student can spell-check his words before programming them into the grid and has a model of the spellings to help with the search. He is then able to participate fully in a group exercise although, possibly, more slowly than his peers.
- Computer 'games', albeit educational ones, are deemed to be 'fun' by students of all ages which can be motivational for the reluctant reader or writer.
- A great deal of software is multisensory; words and information are reinforced by graphics and sound and in many cases the student can use the mouse to move words and objects.
- The student can self-correct errors. The student may be more likely to experiment with language or ideas if he can self-correct on a non-judgemental computer rather than having to present the teacher with a constant round of drafts to be corrected.
- The range of specialist software for dyslexic students of all ages ranging from word and number games to mind mapping software is rapidly increasing.
- The management of the use of ICT can be beneficial to the student. A secondary school had invested in a good range of ICT equipment and software for its learning support department. Supervision was arranged for half of the lunch break during which the students receiving support could access the educational software. They were allowed to bring one friend with the proviso that inappropriate

behaviour from any student meant that this privilege was withdrawn for that student for a set period. This precipitated a learning environment whereby students chose to learn in their 'spare' time, materials were controlled by the supervisor and any stigma regarding attendance of study support was dispelled as other students could use the facilities.

- Older students who have problems with organization find it easier to organize files on a computer than in a folder full of separate sheets of paper, any or all of which can also get lost. Unfortunately, if memory sticks or discs are lost, all of the students work may be lost. The student should develop the habit of ensuring that all work is backed up. While it is preferable to encourage students towards independent learning and responsibility, it may be necessary for the teacher to keep a copy of the work.
- Older students who use a computer on a daily basis may find that using the diary or calendar facilities on a computer can help those with memory or time management difficulties.
- Using specialist software, size of letters, font and background colour can be changed to make reading and writing easier for students with visual problems. Similarly the advent of speech-recognition and text to speech packages has enabled many students who find extreme difficulty with reading to access a much broader range of materials.
- Personal recording machines (dictaphones) can be used for note-taking and planning. Teachers, support staff and parents are often willing to record whole texts so that the student can access these aurally.

Disadvantages of the use of ICT

- Students who experience problems with motor skills may find typing difficult.
- Those with memory difficulties may take time to remember the layout of a keyboard which will slow the process.
- Many educational games and websites are colourfully illustrated which may cause visual disturbance or discomfort. Similarly, older students may find the size or font of text gives rise to similar problems. Software such as 'ReadAble' (see details below) can help.
- It is easy for the teacher to miss persistent errors if these are erased. Classroom and specialist teachers will need to assess errors in order that effective remediation can be planned.
- There is a danger that valuable personal interaction will be lost if the student is working independently. The dyslexic student with low self-esteem may be reluctant to ask for help and may struggle with the task. Interaction is vitally important when working with the dyslexic student as the teacher can learn a great deal about the thought processes the student is employing to complete a task. Ensure that time is spent with the student while he is working on a computer.
- One of the benefits of using a computer is that it is non-judgemental. This also means that it cannot praise apart from giving a typed or spoken 'well done' when a correct answer is given. The teacher can praise effort or for smaller steps taken which will enhance self-esteem.
- Some educational games have instructions whose language is far more advanced than that contained in the game.
- Schools with limited budgets may find it difficult to provide a broad range of software.

Software and assistive technology for the dyslexic student

It would impossible for this book to be completely up-to-date with the latest software and assistive technology available due to the rapidly increasing range of hardware and software on the market.

It is therefore advisable to contact your local authority advisers or specialist suppliers for advice. Iansyst are suppliers who also provide an excellent advisory service. However, it is possible to give an overview of the types of software and other products available, I have included examples that have been tried and trusted favourites of mine and my colleagues.

Reading and spelling:
Chatback (auditory discrimination)
Phonomena (phonological awareness)
Rocketreader (reading speed)
Wordshark (many aspects of reading and spelling)
Eyetrack (visual discrimination and memory)
The Nessy series (many aspects of reading and spelling).

Study skills:
Lucid memory booster (mastering memory ages 5–14)
Scally's World of Problems (sequencing)
Nessy's Brain Book (teenagers and adults).

Maths:
Millie's Maths House (early number work)
Numbershark (general maths)
Mathmania (ages 7–11 and 13–14)
Numbers Up! (older teens and adults)
MathPad for Dragon is now available. This is an addition to the Dragon range of speech recognition software and allows the student to do arithmetic by voice (recommended for secondary age and adult use).

Concept mapping/mind mapping:
Inspiration
Kidspiration (up to age 11)
Mindgenius.

Cross curricular:
Subject specialist publishers may stock software that is suitable or adaptable for dyslexic students. Iansyst carry a small range.

Speech recognition:
The Dragon range
MathPad for Dragon (enables students to do arithmetic by voice).

Text to speech:
textHELP Screen reader V4
The Read and Write range.

Visual stress:
ReadAble (alters the background colour and font) and is now also available in portable form.

Portable writing tools:
Electronic dictionary
Spell-checker
Portable word processor (Alpha Smart is a popular example)
Reading Pen Plus (Oxford dictionary) (scans, displays, reads aloud and defines words)
QuickLink-Pen Elite (allows student to collect notes electronically from printed text).

Voice recorders:
Digital voice recorders
Micro-cassette recorders.

6 The impact of dyslexia on numeracy skills

'I'm still on the words'

This chapter is intended to give an understanding of the nature of the impact of dyslexia on maths and numeracy skills and some strategies that you may wish to use or adapt for your classroom and individual students.

Despite the sterling teaching, research, publications and public awareness carried out in the field of dyslexia and numeracy by Ashcroft, Butterworth, Chinn, Clayton, Henderson, Kay, Sharma, Yeo et al., there are still many teachers, parents and students who are unaware that dyslexia may impact on numeracy and maths skills. Crucially, many teachers and support staff have commented that they do not feel as 'equipped' to support students with numeracy difficulties as literacy difficulties. Media articles and discussion will focus far more often on the impact of dyslexia on literacy than on numeracy, despite the two skill areas being given equal status in the statutory education and Lifelong Learning sectors. Despite my love of number, I have not counted the number of publications and teaching programmes that predominantly cater for literacy difficulties but I would estimate that the number is far higher than that for numeracy.

Research into incidence of students with dyslexia who experience difficulty with mathematics gives varying results. Anne Mitchell (source: ddig.lboro.ac.uk) quotes the following: '60 per cent have significant problems with arithmetic and maths (Joffe, L. 1980)' and '40 per cent have difficulty with mathematics (Butterworth 1999)'. Either statistic indicates a significant number of students with potential difficulties. Working on the accepted figure that 10 per cent of the population is affected by dyslexia to some degree, between 4 per cent and 6 per cent of the population will have difficulty with maths. The mathematician reading this chapter will probably have already calculated that these statistics suggest that she may expect 1 or 2 students in each class to experience difficulties with maths due to dyslexia.

In Chapter 3, Figure 4 looked at the skills needed for effective verbal and written communication. Figure 10 takes a similar view of the skills needed for effective maths learning.

Reading and comprehension	Auditory and visual processing	Self-esteem/confidence	Awareness of learning style	Organization
Visuomotor skills				Concept of number
Motor skills		Maths Learning		Transference of skills
Concentration				Verbal reasoning skills
Auditory and visual memory				Non-verbal reasoning skills
Ability to express ideas in writing	Understanding of concepts/linking concepts	Ability to think in abstract	Recall from long-term memory	Sequencing, direction, spatial awareness

Figure 10 Skills needed for effective maths learning

An investigation into the processes needed to answer a simple mental arithmetic question can highlight how weaknesses in any of these skills areas can prove to be problematic for a student with dyslexia. 'Thirty-five plus twenty-six' appears to be a simple calculation. However, the student first has to remember five separate words and retain these in his short-term memory which may present as the first problem. He then has to 'match' the words 'thirty-five' and 'twenty-six' with the corresponding numbers and hold those. The meaning of word 'add' has to be retrieved from his memory bank and correctly matched to the operation required. At this point, the student who has weak memory skills may have forgotten which operation he has been asked to carry out. The numbers then have to be added. In this case, depending on his thinking style, two sets of numbers or numbers 'carried over' have to be remembered. The figures then have to be turned back into words, again having to match the numbers with words. There is the possibility, during this process, that the student experiencing sequencing problems may transpose the numbers in his head. Finally, he must retrieve the sounds of these words to give an answer verbally. This task demonstrates the scope of the human processing ability but, for the student with dyslexia, one that is prone to error during any one of the processes.

Case study

'I'm still on the words' may appear to be a contradictory subtitle for a chapter on numeracy. It arises from the following incident which, I feel, encapsulates difficulties faced by some dyslexic students and is a phrase that I always keep in the back of my mind when teaching numeracy and maths to students with dyslexia.

During awareness training, a group of study support tutors were asked to add 36 and 25 in their heads and to hold the calculation in their heads. They were then asked to describe how they had arrived at their answer. The object of the exercise was to demonstrate different thinking styles and the comments of the individual members showed an expected mix of inchworms and grasshoppers. However, at the beginning of the discussion, a voice was heard to say 'I'm still on the words'. John, one of the tutors, is dyslexic and he explained to the group that, in the time that they had taken to complete the process successfully and start the discussion, he had only been able to translate the words into number. During this process, he had also forgotten the instruction 'add'.

This anecdote, although involving adult learners, is significant as John, when in the company of other adults whom he knew well, was willing to share this information in order to give his colleagues an insight into the nature of his difficulties. He explained that, as soon as he realized that he would have to undertake this task, he could feel himself begin to panic as he had developed a lifelong fear of being 'put on the spot' with regards to mental arithmetic. He added that he would not have had the confidence, as a child, to explain his difficulty to a teacher and feels that he was deemed to be 'slow'. His self-perception, during his statutory education career, was that he was 'no good at maths', despite being able to understand mathematical concepts, and neither sought nor was offered support. Liebeck (1984) states the 'adults who say "I can't do maths", are usually found to have formed this opinion by the age of eleven. If you don't like something, you tend to avoid it and perhaps fear it'. The fear of failure cycle (Chapter 1) is hard to break. Many dyslexic adult learners have commented that they found that maths learning at school, which was focused on accurate results, was far more stressful than other subjects. This group felt that, whilst they may be able to produce an acceptable written answer to a question in other subject areas, albeit one that they may not have felt demonstrated their true ability, errors made in the process of reaching an answer to a maths question invariably led to an incorrect answer. Being able to answer only half of the questions on a page and the embarrassment of struggling to find a swift answer under the scrutiny of his peers is detrimental to the student's perception of his self-worth.

John's experience of maths, along with that of Nabil (see Chapter 2 – 'Thinking styles in maths') also highlights the fact that some dyslexic students may be good at mathematics but poor at number. Too often, difficulties with number are perceived to indicate poor mathematical ability. If this perception is transmitted to the student, they may 'give up' on any chance of success in maths, leading to a lowering of self-esteem, especially if difficulties are causing problems in other subject areas. Herstein (1975) comments 'very often in mathematics the crucial problem is to recognize and discover what are the relevant concepts; once this is accomplished the job may be more than half done' It could be argued that those dyslexic students who are 'right-brained thinkers' need strategies and support to help them to achieve the 'other half of the job'.

> Encouraging the student to explore mathematics successfully using his strengths, preferred thinking and learning styles in an environment where he can demonstrate his knowledge and skills through a variety of media while giving him the tools to accommodate his weakness will usually reap benefits in terms of raising self-esteem, enthusiasm and attainment.

Dyscalculia

The word dyscalculia derives from the Greek word '*dys*' and the Latin word '*calculare*' and means 'difficulty with counting'. '*Calculare*' is derived from '*calculus*' which was one of a number of small stones used to make an abacus.

The debate as to whether dyscalculia could be 'labelled' as a specific learning difficulty as distinct from those difficulties with number encountered by the dyslexic student continued for some time. The current consensus is that while dyscalculia and dyslexia can exist independently, there may be co-morbidity (a student may have dyscalculia and dyslexia).

The Department for Education and Skills (DfES) (2007) defines dyscalculia as 'A condition that affects the ability to acquire arithmetical skills. Dyscalculic learners may have difficulty understanding simple number concepts, lack an intuitive grasp of numbers, and have problems learning number facts and procedures. Even if they produce a correct answer or use a correct method, they may do so mechanically and without confidence' (Source: The National Numeracy Strategy: Guidance to Support Pupils with Dyslexia and Dyscalculia).

The guidance continues: 'dyscalculia appears to be a difference relating specifically to number. This means that dyscalculic learners do not have the difficulties with language that are associated with dyslexia'.

The subject of dyscalculia is fascinating and worth further investigation than a book of this size has room for. Suggestions for further reading on dyslexia and maths and dyscalculia can be found at the end of this book.

Assessment

I am often asked if a dyslexic student is also dyscalculic or if his dyslexia is impacting on maths skills. At present, there is still much work being carried out in the field of assessment for dyscalculia. Consequently, my usual response to this question is that I find it more productive to assess where difficulties lie and to help the student to accommodate these rather than trying to label students.

Obviously there will be a number of students who experience difficulties solely with number (as noted in the second quotation above) whose literacy skills would not have given cause for concern and who would not, consequently, have been assessed. Some schools may deem it necessary to carry out a separate assessment for dyscalculia and may wish to invest in the Dyscalculia Screener (for ages 6–14) devised by Brian Butterworth which is a computer-based screener. However, the maths teacher can use attainment scores from class assessments and keep notes of difficulties encountered in the classroom to act as evidence that the student may need support with number. There are paper-based assessment materials such as the Mathematics Competency Test (for ages 11 to adult) which can indicate difficulty in four specific areas, using and applying mathematics, number and algebra, shape and space and handling data. The DfES Standards Site states that 'it is not a bad idea' for the teacher to set up her own informal diagnosis and cites the example of one Local Education Authority who based this on suggestions in Chapter 3 of Steve Chinn's book *Mathematics for Dyslexics: A Teaching Handbook*. This should include discussion with the student as to how he arrived at his answers which will give an indication of learning and thinking styles as well as highlighting potential underlying areas of difficulty. The Standards Site puts this quite succinctly: 'Remember, the errors are more revealing than the correct answers. The end result of a mathematics test should be a lot more than just a number'. A formal diagnostic assessment for dyslexia will include a maths assessment. This will help the assessor to build a picture of the impact of dyslexia on numeracy skills or the possibility of the presence of dyscalculia if concerns from maths teachers are included in background information to the assessment.

I also enquire about the student's performance outside the maths classroom from staff in other subject areas. Work involving number occurs in many subject areas including science and technology. The student may have difficulty with measurement in the workshop or kitchen, using ratio to mix paints in art and being able to ascertain quickly whether he has gathered a team of seven during sports lessons. A discussion with the student and, possibly, parents concerning difficulties encountered in everyday life such as counting change, telling the time, reading timetables, setting video recorders can prove enlightening. The younger student who cannot recognize a group of four objects without counting them, cannot recognize commutative numbers and relationships between numbers and cannot count on from numbers without starting at one would also give cause for concern. Assessment is an ongoing process of information gathering from, potentially, a significant number of people.

The following are signs that dyslexia may be impacting on numeracy:

Signs of dyslexia in numeracy

- Slow speed of working.
- Difficulty in remembering number facts, times tables, number bonds and relationships between numbers, commutative numbers.
- Difficulty in remembering formulae, vocabulary and matching symbols to words.
- Forgetting correct processes and sequence of operations or getting lost in a series of operations.
- Needing several explanations of concepts or processes, but is able to complete work successfully once understanding has taken place.
- Cannot do mental arithmetic.
- Transposes, reverses or inverts numbers.
- Misreads or incorrectly writes numbers.
- Difficulty in reading or constructing charts, graphs and tables accurately.
- Miscopies from the board or copies things twice (may copy the answer from a previous question in workbooks).
- May miss decimal points.
- Confuses words when listening and speaking.
- Difficulty in decoding vocabulary.
- Difficulty with comprehension in worded problems.
- Misinterpreting or not attempting worded exam questions.
- Misinterpretation of maths words in everyday use (e.g. product).
- Difficulty with practical tasks (measuring, drawing, using equipment).
- Poor presentation of work.
- Difficulties with place value, ordering number.
- Cannot do elapsed time/read timetables.
- Starts at the 'wrong end' during computation.
- Visual difficulties associated with Meares-Irlen (distortion of figures, difficulties with reading, discomfort when using squared paper).

Turning concrete to abstract

'Mathematical insights are very seldom generated on blackboards.' (Dienes 1960)

This comment still holds true today and successions of mathematicians, academics and teachers have researched, practised and published their theories on the benefits of a more active approach to maths learning. The QIA (Quality

Improvement Agency) have a range of teaching and learning resources, 'Improving Learning in Mathematics' which demonstrates the benefits of active learning. I would recommend a visit to the website (http://teachingandlearning.qia.org.uk).

Sharma (1989, cited in 'Developmental Perspectives on Dyscalculia: Implications for teaching in the middle and secondary school' (available at www.dyscalculia.org/Edu562.html) p.19) argued that the teacher must take each student completely through the six levels of learning mastery of a mathematical concept. The term 'level' refers to the order that mathematical information is processed and learned. These are:

1. Intuitive connection of the new concept to existing knowledge and experiences.
2. Concrete modelling wherein the student looks for concrete material to construct a model or show a manifestation of the concept.
3. Pictorial or representational, where the student draws to illustrate the concept and so connects the concrete or vividly imagined example to the symbolic picture or representation.
4. Abstract or symbolic, where the student translates the concept into mathematical notation using number symbols, operational signs, formulas, and equations.
5. Application, where the student applies the concept successfully to real-world situations, story problems and projects.
6. Communication: The student can teach the concept successfully to others or can communicate it on a test. Students can be paired up to teach one another the concept.

Many adults will remember maths teaching as consisting largely of steps 1 and 4 in Sharma's model whereby students were expected to carry out and solve written problems after a 'chalk and talk' explanation. For many students this was not conducive to their learning styles and it is not uncommon to hear adults bemoan the fact that maths was 'boring' or 'impossible to understand'. The National Numeracy Strategy (1998) advocated greater use of representational material but, for some dyslexic students, this still does not facilitate understanding. The dyslexic student would then be given concrete materials to help him to understand the concept. This is an unsatisfactory situation for several reasons. The use of concrete materials when other students are not using these may single out the dyslexic student from his peers or the student may feel that he has failed, both of which will be detrimental to self-esteem. The student may have spent a great deal of time attempting to understand the concept using pictorial representation and will have to repeat this part of the process after working with concrete materials. The back and forth change, rather than a progression, may cause confusion for the dyslexic student as it may be hard for him, when revisiting the pictorial representation, to dismiss his earlier misinterpretation.

The important work of Chinn and Ashcroft recognized that the weaknesses in cognitive skills such as memory and processing common in many dyslexic students often contributed to 'failure' in maths. Yeo (2003) explains the argument propounded by Chinn and Ashcroft thus: 'Dyslexic children with maths learning difficulties should be given access to concrete materials and concrete materials should be used to help children make sense of all of the conceptual and calculation aspects of maths. They made clear that many individual Dyslexic children benefit from using concrete materials at critical points throughout their maths learning careers'.

Sahlberg and Berry (2002) state that 'researchers have suggested a shift from teacher-centred instruction towards more active participatory learning methods as one way to improve the quality of the learning process'. It would appear that this line of reasoning is now being adopted. The revised National Numeracy Strategy (2006) in the 'Framework for Teaching Maths from Reception to Year 6' makes reference to 'activities', 'practical activities' and 'real-life problems'.

Students of all ages studying maths and numeracy at all levels should have the opportunity to explore mathematics using what appears to be the most effective order of processes.

> **The needs of the dyslexic student can be more effectively accommodated in a student-centred active learning process which can help to reduce the possibility of him 'giving up' through constant fear of failure.**

Multisensory resources in the maths classroom

Multisensory resources or visual aids should be an integral part of lessons for all ages of student. However, the situation in which these are used is important. As noted in the previous section, a student may feel patronized if he, as one student commented, 'is the only one using baby equipment'. This can lead to a lowering of self-esteem and the possibility of teasing from other students. It must also be remembered that all students may struggle with the understanding of particular concepts or aspects of computation at any point in their mathematical career and the use of such resources can also be of help to them.

A cupboard, box or portable trolley containing the resources listed below can be kept in the classroom. At the beginning of the year this can be introduced as a resource for *all* students in the class to use when the student himself feels that this will aid the learning process. In this way, resources become student-centred rather than teacher-centred. This will encourage all students to assess what tools may be needed to tackle a problem and will help the dyslexic student to develop strategies independently to help him accommodate his difficulties. The dyslexic student will feel far less reluctant to use equipment if this is viewed as a whole-class resource.

Multisensory resources

- Base Ten materials (Dienes Blocks)
- Multilink cubes
- Counters
- Blank playing cards
- Cuisenaire rods
- Flexitables
- Plastic numbers
- Geoboards
- 3-dimensional shapes
- Measuring equipment
- Fraction 'pies' or blocks
- Shape templates
- Calculators
- Coins/plastic money.

Visual aids

- Multiplication squares
- Addition squares
- 100 squares
- Place value charts
- Equivalent fraction charts
- Squared paper
- Number lines.

In addition, everyday objects and general classroom materials such as paper, scissors, straws, clay, cards can all be used by students to explore, experiment and demonstrate.

There is now a vast range of computer software ranging from early number games to individual programmes to help with creating and solving equations. A list of suggested software is given in the ICT section of this book.

Ten pieces of equipment that cannot be kept in a box are the student's fingers; many dyslexic students need to use their fingers to help with calculation. Younger students will openly use this vital resource but many older students can be seen surreptitiously counting on their fingers under the table or may be too 'embarrassed' to be seen to be working in this way. I introduce and display this sign (Figure 11) as a reminder to students that this way of working is acceptable.

Nature's Calculator

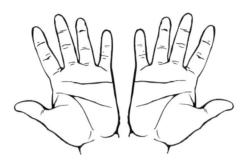

Please use in this room!

Figure 11 Nature's calculator

A resource is most effective when it is appropriate for the needs of the individual student at a particular time or for a particular purpose. If a Year 9 student is still having difficulty with the concept of volume, he may be encouraged to investigate the use of multilink cubes. The crucial words here are 'encouraged' and 'investigate'. Materials should be used by the student to help him to explore and understand concepts. He should be able to understand why he is using that particular resource and use it as an effective part of his investigation. Demonstration of materials by the teacher should be in discussion with the student not given to the student.

There are numerous examples of the use of multisensory materials in the publications recommended at the end of this book. Many innovative uses of materials are being explored in schools around the country. There are now opportunities for teachers to share ideas, one of which is the website of the National Centre for Excellence in the Teaching of Mathematics (NCETM). NCETM states that it 'is developing a sustainable national infrastructure for subject-specific professional development for teachers of mathematics. This is a vital part of strengthening the teaching and learning of mathematics; it will realize the mathematical potential of learners and raise the status of the profession'. Partners in Education UK Ltd (www.partnersineducation.co.uk) are an excellent source of materials for students with specific learning difficulties

Case study

This case study shows a very simple but effective use of equipment which opened up a whole area of maths for the particular student.

Andrea, a Year 11 student, made consistent errors in or could not attempt questions concerning volume in GCSE practice papers. Her teacher could not decide whether she was experiencing difficulty in understanding the wording of problems set or had a basic problem with the concept of volume.

She was given this simple problem to solve:

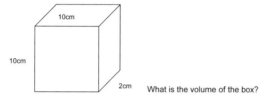

Figure 12

Her answer was 102cm^2.

Andrea had understood the concepts of linear and 2-dimensional measurement. She had grasped the concept of squaring by carrying out the multisensory experiment of drawing lines and counting boxes and had demonstrated to her teacher that she had progressed to calculating area without drawing lines. Andrea was asked how she arrived at her answer to the question. Andrea could not visualize the drawing as a 3-dimensional figure. She managed to calculate 10 cm x 10cm to arrive at 100cm^2. She then became totally confused as to what to do with the 2cm figure. As this was a straight line, she added it to her existing total as she had viewed this as a linear measurement and tried to add it as she would have done when calculating perimeter. During her explanation, Andrea realized that she could not add linear and squared measurements, but could not move forward with the problem. She was given Dienes Blocks to experiment with and quickly constructed a concrete representation of the figure which enabled her to gain understanding of the concept of volume and operations needed to gain a correct answer to the problem. Andrea was quickly able to move to more complex problems involving volume, including worded questions and reported that believed that she successfully answered similar questions on her GCSE paper.

A dyslexic student may have gained greater familiarity with these resources through use during individual support sessions and will be able to demonstrate potential usage to his peers, making him an invaluable member of his peer group which, in turn, may help raise his self-esteem.

The most important multisensory resources are the students themselves. In his article 'Towards more active learning approaches' (2007), Malcolm Swann describes the Standard Units Maths Project approach to the use of posters:

> Posters are often used in schools and colleges to display the finished, polished work of learners. In our work, however, we use them to promote collaborative thinking. The posters are not produced at the end of the learning activity; they are the learning activity and they show all the thinking that has taken place 'warts and all'. We often ask learners to solve a problem in two different ways on the poster and then display the results for other learners to comment on.

On considering the active learning aspects of this task if this is carried out as a paired or group activity, I viewed this description with regards to the potential impact on the learning of the dyslexic student:

- The dyslexic student is looking at what the other students are doing, listening to students' thoughts and ideas, verbally participating in discussion and making his own contribution to the physical construction of the poster.
- He can accommodate his strengths and weaknesses seamlessly. For example, the student with poor motor skills or one who has difficulty in reading or recording written work can leave these tasks to other members of the group and concentrate on other ways to input effectively into the activity.
- Students are initially giving concrete representation of existing skills upon which they build. The dyslexic student may not have grasped an abstract concept but may be able to use his peers' concrete representation of their knowledge to gain sufficient understanding to enable him to progress.
- Students' thinking styles are exhibited and discussed. This promotes an exchange of thinking styles amongst the students and allows the teacher to gain further insight into the students' individual styles.
- The 'warts and all' approach is invaluable to the dyslexic student's self-esteem. He realizes that, not only may his ways of thinking and solving problems be valued by his peers, but that others can experience difficulty with aspects of maths investigation.
- This uses very little 'equipment'. More importantly, the use of equipment in the learning experience is driven by the students, not the other way around.

One Early Years teacher uses dance to teach direction and counting. She advises that current articles on the internet indicate that dance and music may be more important than the use of ICT for securing learning. She also pointed out that dance and music may appeal to the more creative side of the dyslexic student and provide a 'handle' for him to link mathematical concepts with things that he can experience and understand at a very early age. I do not have an example to give of the use of music within the secondary school maths classroom but I am certain that innovative maths teachers have explored this possibility. Collaborative work with the music department could involve a group of students producing recorded versions of 'times tables to music' in their preferred style of music.

I have learned a great deal about how dyslexic students learn and have looked at some maths concepts from a different angle by listening to students explain how they use resources. I have suggested their strategies to other students. However, it is extremely important to recognize that not all multisensory equipment will be suitable for all dyslexic students. It is also important that the teacher uses materials that she feels comfortable with.

Areas of impact

Memory

Typical difficulties:

- Students with weak short-term memories will often have difficulty in remembering strings of instructions. When a teacher asks a student to look at a question in a textbook, for example, the obvious statement would be 'open your books, turn to page 36 and look at Question 4'. What she is in fact giving are three instructions (open, turn, look) and three pieces of information (books, page 36 and Question 4). Those with the most severe memory problems may only get as far as opening the book. It may help to avoid giving obvious information such as 'open the book' as this still has to be processed by the student. Ask the student to turn to page 36 before giving the question number. It is not uncommon for the dyslexic student to be constantly referring to what his neighbour is doing.
- Homework may be written down incorrectly and equipment needed for the next lesson may be forgotten.
- Information may be lost during explanation of concepts. This has often gone unrecognized as a problem with memory as it may be believed that the student has not understood the concept when, in fact, they may have forgotten part of what has been said and have tried to 'fill in the gaps'.
- Poor auditory memory skills will not support the retention of great amounts of information delivered verbally.
- Poor visual memory means that the student may not remember written information.
- The student may lose concentration and 'switch off'. They may be deemed to be 'lazy' or 'uninterested'.
- Long-term memory problems can lead to difficulty in remembering and retrieving number bonds, number facts and times tables. This can present from a young age but may persist throughout the student's life. When considering that there are 81 combinations of numbers from 1–9 (including demonstration of commutable numbers) and 100 numbers in a 10 x 10 multiplication square it is easy to imagine the difficulty encountered by a student trying to remember these facts. Miles (1992) states 'almost all dyslexic pupils have difficulties in learning their tables and reciting them'.
- Relying on insecure memory skills can not only lead to errors in computation but can disrupt the flow of

working. I have witnessed the frustration of many students who have been unable to enjoy maths exploration due to being 'bogged down' in the computation.

Strategies

- General strategies to help with memory can be found in Chapter 3.
- Cuisenaire rods are an excellent multisensory way of looking at the relationship between numbers when working on number bonds. When progressing to symbolic representation, playing cards with numbers can be manipulated to help with understanding of commutative numbers.
- Display multiplication squares and addition squares displayed on classroom walls (primary and secondary) for reinforcement.
- Students can complete a multiplication square and stick it into the front of their maths workbooks (ensure that there is a model to copy or to check accuracy).
- Most students will remember two, five and ten-times tables. Use this as a base for students to calculate other numbers. For example, to calculate 6 x 7, the student can use his 'base' knowledge that 5 x 7 = 35 then add a further 7.
- Use 'times tables to music' tapes or CDs.
- There are many excellent games available to help with reinforcement of tables (Partners in Education UK Ltd stock an inexpensive game that has proved very popular with students of all ages).
- Do not discourage students' own techniques. I have seen 4 x 8 calculated as 8 + 8 = 16, 16 + 8 = 24, 24 + 8 = 32 (each step using fingers to add). Another student gave 8 x 2 = 16, 16 +16 = 32. Neither student could accurately recall the fact 8 x 4 = 32 but both, using their methods, could arrive at a correct answer during calculations albeit at a slower speed than their peers.
- Allow the use of fingers for calculation. Students often use fingers to calculate the nine times table. The picture below shows the student calculating 3 x 9. The third finger (thumbs are included) is held down. The fingers to the left represent tens (in this case 20) and the fingers to the right represent units (in this case 7). The student then calculates that 3 x 9 = 27.

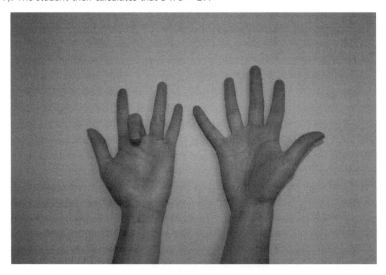

Figure 13

- Students may not remember the relationship between numbers (50%, 0.5, 1/2). Again, students can construct charts to be used for revision and reference.
- Students of all ages may find difficulty in matching terminology to symbols. There is a section in *Maths for the Dyslexic. A Practical Guide* by Anne Henderson in which she describes her use of diagrammatic connections. A student, Rajiv, adapted this idea and, using his ICT skills, produced this diagram.

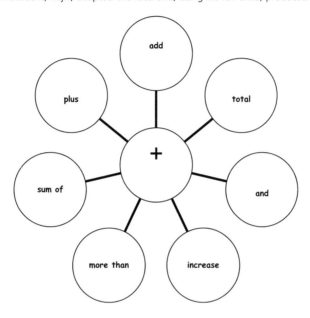

Figure 14 Rajiv's diagram

Rajiv began with the two words 'add' and 'plus' and saved these on the computer. He could then use this as a working document to build his bank of vocabulary. He printed amended copies and kept them in an exercise book for referral. Rajiv repeated this exercise with −, ÷, x and =.

There is great potential for adapting this as an organic whole-class or group exercise. Students can construct their own posters which can be displayed on classroom walls and used as 'works in process' in which the vocabulary bank is expanded as students meet new words. The dyslexic student can derive considerable benefit from this type of work. He can have a productive input into group discussion as to the design of a poster, assist in the practical aspects of the production, will gain understanding and overlearning of the terminology through group discussion and can use the ongoing display to act as reference and reinforcement.

- Personal dictionaries can be compiled. Discuss the most suitable layout for the student; some may wish this to be in alphabetical order, others will prefer this to be under topic headings. Encourage the student to write his own definition as this reinforces understanding and research has shown that individuals are more likely to remember their own words and phrases. If the student has a slow reading speed, definitions can be brief, in bullet-point form or pictorial representations for easy access. These can be used as reference throughout the year and for revision.
- *Maths Dictionary* by Peter Robson contains clear, concise definitions and explanations of terms, many of which are illustrated by simple diagrams. This is an accessible and inexpensive book which could be used to help the student devise his own definitions. If the student wishes to use this book as reference,

I would still suggest that this is personalized and that he identifies and highlights those terms that he may forget.

- The student can make memory cards for formulae. The subject (e.g. area of a circle) is written on one side and the formula on the other. Ensure that the student who has organizational problems stores these in a format that is easily accessible.
- Vocabulary cards can be displayed on classroom walls. This could be done as a whole-class exercise. Some students with poor working memories do not realize that they have forgotten terminology. Displayed words can act as a reminder.
- Use visual 'pegs'. Students can draw shapes and write the names inside the shape (not underneath as it is harder to visualize the whole picture). Encourage students to remember practical or visual demonstrations.
- Use 'words within words' or word association. 'Perimeter' includes the word 'rim'. A capital D looks like a semi-circle and the 'stick' is therefore the diameter, so D = diameter.
- Promote the understanding rather than the remembering of concepts and processes.
- Give models of processes for the student to follow.
- Simplify where possible. Students try to remember (usually with little success):

    + x + = +
    - x - = +
    - x + = -
    + x - = -

    If the student remembers 'like signs are positive' all of the rest follows.
- Students often forget the meanings of vocabulary and terminology which can lead to misinterpretation of written and verbal information or the inability to solve or carry out a worded problem or calculation. This can cause frustration within the classroom and could have a significant impact during examinations. Many dyslexic students also experience considerable difficulty with remembering formulae and processes.

Case study

Sanjay, a Year 5 student, had severe memory problems and, despite excellent teaching and one-on-one support, remembered very little of previously learned concepts. He was experiencing difficulty with remembering words connected with shape. There happened to be an ant on the classroom floor. It was pointed out to Sanjay that the word 'perimeter' contained the word 'rim'. Sanjay was asked to imagine the ant walking around the rim of the drawing of a square. The ant, quickly named 'Rimmer', spent the rest of the morning walking around the perimeter of the window, whiteboard, books and various other objects within the room which were subsequently measured and recorded. When revisiting the topic in Year 6, Sanjay immediately stated 'Rimmer can walk around the perimeter again'.

Revision

Revision periods can be an extremely stressful for dyslexic students. Many view maths as particularly 'taxing' on the memory due to the amount of processes, formulae and number facts to be remembered. Students have arrived at support sessions in a state of considerable distress as they have tried to memorize whole maths textbooks afresh regardless of whether any of the information was already retained. It is quite common for revision to appear 'ineffective' despite hours of work.

Strategies

- A student can compile his own revision notebook. He can be advised, initially, to look at topics and note what he cannot remember. This has the dual effect of enabling the student to revise the topic as he is writing it and to appreciate how much he already knows which can greatly reduce stress levels. The whole topic, including the recently revised material, can then be revised as a whole.
- Remind the student to use dictionaries, memory cards and vocabulary cards for revision.
- As with any other subject area, revision should be carried out in short sections and frequent rest breaks allowed to avoid information overload.
- The use of pictures linked to descriptions may help – for example, draw an ant and rectangle, then write 'perimeter' and 'Rimmer' (see case study above).

Processing

Difficulties

- Processing difficulties can affect both speed and accuracy of working. In the case study of John his slow speed of processing meant that he was 'still on the words' long after his colleagues had completed a simple mental arithmetic calculation and were discussing the results. In the process of trying to turn words into numbers in his head, he forgot the instruction to add the numbers so would not have been able to carry out the computation.
- A slow speed of working can be as frustrating for the dyslexic student as it can be for the teacher.
- The student, when given a set number of questions to answer within the class, will be very aware that he will probably not be able to complete as many as his peers which may lead to a lack of self-esteem.
- If a set of questions is designed so that they become progressively more complex or test extended knowledge, the student may not have the opportunity to demonstrate, and the teacher will not be able to evaluate fully, the extent of his understanding of a topic.
- The student will probably find mental arithmetic problems extremely difficult.

Strategies

- Where possible, allow extra time for the completion of work. Do not try to 'rush' the dyslexic student as he is likely to make errors under pressure.
- Expect less work in the classroom. If it is deemed that the student may be capable of completing the full range of a set of questions, ask him do samples at each level (e.g. alternate questions). As dyslexic

students become more aware of the impact of dyslexia on learning, many realize that they will have to spend far longer than their peers to complete work, including homework. The dedication of many dyslexic students and their determination to succeed means that, despite not being able to carry out as much work in the classroom as their peers, they will wish to complete the same amount of homework. A discussion may need to take place with any or all of the students, SENCO and parent/carer to ascertain the amount of work that the student can reasonably cope with.

- Avoid putting students 'on the spot' by asking mental arithmetic questions that expect an answer delivered verbally. Group use of individual whiteboards, whereby all students write an answer and show this to the teacher is a far better way of demonstrating understanding for the dyslexic student who will be able to manipulate numbers that they can see. Incorrect answers can be erased; permanent records of errors can be very dispiriting for the dyslexic student.

- If calculation is not the skill being tested during a topic and slow speed is hindering the flow of exploration, allow the use of calculators and multiplication squares so that the student can fully engage in the task.

- The student may need several explanations of concepts or processes before understanding is securely processed. The student who has weak auditory memory and processing problems will find particular difficulty with explanations delivered verbally.

- He may experience disruption to concentration if he is overloaded with information that he cannot process.

- Even when the student has demonstrated understanding of a process and the ability to apply this successfully, he may still get lost during the process. This has obvious implications during examinations, particularly when the student has difficulty in processing questions presented as long sentences (see 'Reading' section below).

- Some students may get 'lost' during a complex series of processes. Many find themselves trying to 'backtrack' over work in order that this may act as a memory prompt for the next step. This is time consuming and may also add to the confusion.

- Ensure that the student has sufficient time to practise and master concepts. If the student receives support or if it is possible to request support, ensure that there is effective communication between the teacher and support staff to enable reinforcement of a topic to be current, pertinent and effective.

- When a student is working independently, check that he is on track with the process that he is working on. Group work can greatly help as the student can give productive input into the group while following the group's train of thought and work.

- Multisensory exploration will help as the student can use his stronger skills to help process the information. It is important that the student is encouraged to explore and understand processes to support memory. In this way he may be able to 'work out' the next stage of a process rather than have to rely on memory. Allow for lapses of concentration.

- Give models of processes for reference.

- If a student is thought to have a grasshopper thinking style, encourage him to estimate a final result and to keep this in mind. It may help him to view the processes as part of a whole and he may be better able to visualize the sequence of processes.

- Many students, especially those whose self-perception is that they are 'no good' at maths, will state that they are unable to carry out lengthy calculations. Instil the idea that, allowing that the student understands the principles of addition, then $342678 + 45329$ is not 'harder' than $34 + 56$. There is simply more work to do. I have found that many students have not attempted examination questions through being overwhelmed by 'large' numbers and have lacked the confidence to attempt calculation.

- Use acronyms such as BIDMAS (Brackets Indices Division Multiplication Addition Subtraction) to help remember sequences of processes. Encourage the student to create his own for other processes. A word of caution; students with weak memory skills may forget the acronym.
- The student may qualify for extra time during examinations. Check with the SENCO or exams office whether this is in place. If not, express concerns to the SENCO who will be able to arrange for an Access Arrangement assessment.

Case study

> Rebecca's Year 5 teacher played 'round the world' multiplication games with the class. This involves sitting students in a circle with one member of the group standing behind another. The two students are given a multiplication task and the first to give a correct answer then becomes or remains the person standing up and moves onto the next student. When one student successfully manages to remain standing after 'beating' all members of the circle he has gone 'round the world' and is the winner. Most students, over time, usually get a turn at 'standing up' or will give an answer even if they are not the first to do so. Rebecca could never give a swift response as she had a slow speed of processing and became tearful whenever this game was suggested. As it was sometimes difficult to decide which student had answered first, she took on the role of 'judge' which meant that she could take an active role in the game but was not required to participate in the questioning.

Reading

Difficulties

- Students may experience difficulty in decoding subject-specific vocabulary and may also misread similar-looking words such as 'diameter' for 'diagram'.
- Words used in maths may have other meanings in everyday life; a product is something advertised on television, you take away fast food and a degree is something that your teacher has.
- Some dyslexic students have difficulty with the past tense. 'John had 17 apples on his tree. He gave 4 to Jane. How many did he have?' The answer would appear to be 13 until the question 'Did he have 17 apples before or after he gave 4 to Jane?' arises.
- Comprehension difficulties with worded explanations and questions pose significant problems for some students, particularly during private revision and when reading examination questions. Mis-interpretation of examination questions is common and many students may not even attempt worded questions. One Year 11 student explained that he had given wrong answers to so many worded questions during practice papers and actual exams starting with his SAT tests in Year 6 that he had lost all confidence in his ability to answer correctly worded questions and he had, consequently, 'given up' on these questions. Much of my specialist teaching work with GCSE students has involved working on worded questions as students unable to access these have often found that they can do the maths contained within the questions.
- Often teachers have worked hard to help students to remember mathematics vocabulary and

terminology only to find that it is the everyday words and names used in worded questions that cause difficulty.

Case study

Daniel, a Year 7 student working on area, was presented with the question 'A man had 100 tiles measuring $1m^2$ to build a square patio. How big was the patio?' Daniel could not read the word patio and did not know the meaning of the word when he finally asked for it to be read to him (he had spent approximately 5 minutes trying to decode the word). He had been so engrossed in trying to decode the word and set the problem in an unfamiliar context, that he had lost sight of the key maths words and did not realize that he could have solved the problem without knowing what a patio is.

Strategies

- Students need to develop skimming and scanning techniques to enable them to identify key words to give a gist of what concepts or operations are needed to answer the question. Words can be high-lighted, circled or underlined. This skill takes practice and is often most effective when a demonstration is given by the teacher followed by discussion of further examples. This can be done as a whole-class exercise, becoming the normal way of working for all worded questions, not purely for exam practice, and an interactive whiteboard is the perfect medium with which to do this. Very often, students are not taught these skills until well into secondary education when the dyslexic student may have begun to struggle and lose confidence. If this technique is practised as soon as students encounter worded questions during primary education, dyslexic students would have far greater confidence in tackling worded questions throughout the rest of their maths career.
This example resulted from discussion within a small group of students.
Jasmine went shopping in London with a <u>£50</u> note. She bought a skirt for <u>£4.99</u>, a pair of shoes in the sale for <u>£17.85</u> and a purse for <u>£3.20</u>. <u>Estimate</u> how much <u>change</u> she had <u>left</u>.
- Personal dictionaries can be constructed as outlined earlier in the 'Memory' section.
- Encourage students to remember that names begin with capital letters so if these are seen in a question, it may not be necessary to spend time trying to decode the names. If the names are repeated within the question they can be recognized by the initial or first two letters.
- Ensure that students have a clear understanding of the meaning and application of vocabulary. Use cards to match words to definitions.
- Ask the dyslexic student to give an explanation of a term after you or another student has read the word. This will help with self-esteem as the student can demonstrate knowledge even if he cannot read the word.
- If the student appears to be having significant difficulty with reading, check with the SENCO to ascertain whether they qualify for the services of a reader during examinations. If so, it is recommended that this should be his normal way of working and he may need to have worded information and questions read for him in class.

Visual and auditory discrimination

- Problems with visual discrimination can lead to the student transposing, reversing and inverting numbers. This can happen when both reading and writing numbers, including copying from the board or textbook.
- Symbols also present a problem; + and x can easily be mistaken for the other as can - and ÷.
- Decimal points may be missed.
- If a number is transposed in copying, the student will obviously give the wrong answer to a question despite having carried out a correct calculation of the numbers used.
- The student may also have difficult in accurately reading times tables and constructing graphs, charts and tables.
- He may also experience problems with noting similarities and differences in shapes.
- Students with auditory discrimination may confuse similar-sounding words such as 30/13, reflection/rotation, when listening or speaking. If a word is written incorrectly, there is the potential for a student to give an incorrect answer. It is quite common for the numbers 13 to 19 to be written incorrectly as the student writes what he believes that he hears. 'Fourteen' has two syllables, 'four' and 'teen'. The student knows that 'teen' means ten so may write the syllables in the order that he hears them, which is 41.

Strategies

- Check that information has been correctly copied. Take care that the student has not been given poorly written or photocopied worksheets and that symbols and numbers cannot easily be misinterpreted when written on the board.
- Use squared paper to maximum effect. Encourage the student to use the whole square and write the x sign to the four corners of the square and the + to the middle of the lines.
- Ann Arbor Publishers are a good source of publications and resources to help students with visual discrimination difficulties.
- It may help some students if graphs, tables and figures are enlarged if a book has very closely printed text.
- Discussion regarding the properties of shapes either on a broad or specific basis may help with differentiation.
- Check that the students have correctly heard and written numbers, vocabulary and instructions.
- Students may find multiplication squares visually confusing. 'Flexitables', which are plastic multiplication tables, can be folded along the lines of multiplication to leave the answer at the intersection of the two folds. 100 squares, equivalent number charts, are also produced in Flexitables form and can be obtained from Partners in Education UK Ltd.
- It may not be logistically possible to check everything that a student has written. If visual or auditory discrimination causes significant difficulties, it may be advisable to provide handouts or write for the student. You may need to discuss the availability of support or encourage a 'buddy system' whereby another student could take notes or check that work has been written correctly. As with any use of a buddy system, ensure that this is not a 'one-way street' of assistance and that the student can share other skills with his partner.

Perseveration

Anne Henderson (1998) quotes Professor Miles as describing perseveration as 'rather like a tune that won't go out of your head'. Students may copy earlier numbers or symbols from a board, textbook or their own work. Students who need to refer to a model may often calculate a second example using the correct numbers but will repeat the model answer. It is not unknown for a student to arrive at a whole page of identical answers. It is only when checking the work that he will see his errors.

36 + 43 could become 36 + 36 or 36 + 46.

115		115
326 + could become		115 +
		326

24 + 46 - 7 could become 24 + 46 + 7.

Some students may copy this last question correctly and will use the correct numbers during the calculation but will continue to add rather than subtract the 7.

Strategies

- Use differently coloured whiteboard markers for different stages of the sum (unless you have colour-blind students for whom this may cause problems). This can also help students with processing or tackling problems as it is easier for them to find their place.
- Students who repeat sections of their work or miscopy from textbooks can cover up previous work or lines in a book. Those who need to refer to a model should refer back then cover.
- Encourage the student to check work frequently, especially when older students will be carrying out series of operations.

Meares-Irlen Syndrome

Meares-Irlen Syndrome is described in greater detail in Chapter 3.

Difficulties

- Visual distortion and discomfort may obviously cause difficulty when reading worded problems but numbers and symbols may also be interpreted inaccurately. A 'wobbly' '+' sign could easily turn into a 'x'.
- Many students with Meares-Irlen Syndrome have complained that the use of squared paper causes visual confusion or discomfort. Students have commented that continually moving lines can act as a major disruption to concentration. One student complained that this sort of movement made her 'feel seasick'. She was accustomed to words and figures moving but could not cope with the additional movement of the lines. Other students have described the squares as 'squashing' the numbers.
- Blurred and distorted figures can render working with shape and data handling very difficult.

Strategies

- Use coloured overlays. If the student has had an Intuitive Overlay assessment, a particular colour will have been suggested. This should help with reading and looking at shape and data handling examples. However, the overlay may not stop all of the distortion and he may need help in interpreting charts and diagrams.
- This will not solve the problems that the student may encounter when measuring angles or drawing shapes and constructing graphs, diagrams and tables. Working on coloured paper may help. If the condition is so severe that it prevents the student from achieving in these areas, a discussion with the SENCO may be needed. The student's parents/carers may wish to investigate obtaining tinted lenses or it may be more appropriate for the student to receive support in the class in the form of a scribe who could carry out these practical tasks for him.
- Avoid using squared paper if this causes discomfort.

Sequencing , direction and orientation

Difficulties

Sequencing difficulties can affect learning times tables, number sequences and number patterns. The student may be unable to automatically 'find' numbers in a sequence in the same way that they find difficulty in sequencing the alphabet.

Relationships between numbers may not appear obvious. For example, a student may recognize that the number sequence 2, 4, 6, 8 rises in steps of 2 as this is the basis of the two-times table. He may not recognize that 3, 5, 7 and 9 have the same pattern.

One of the most common areas for error and one that many teachers find the most difficult to manage is starting at the 'wrong end' in calculations. Younger students are taught to add, subtract and multiply from right to left then are faced with working from left to right for division. For some students, the right to left working for the first three operations is secure and difficulties are only encountered in division. For others, especially those for whom this is not secure, the confusion becomes global across the four basic operations.

Most teachers will also have encountered the students who will subtract the 'bottom' number from the 'top'. This can also be compounded by the manner in which the sum is written. Some students may have a lifelong difficulty in calculating figures written in a liner fashion (46 + 35 - 23).

Fractions can also be problematic as the student knows that 6 is larger than 4 but that when these become denominators, $\frac{1}{6}$ is smaller than $\frac{1}{4}$.

Place value is a concept that many students find difficult and yet it is one that plays a crucial part in so many areas of mathematics as are positive and negative numbers which can also prove problematic.

Students may find difficulty with ordering numbers.

Case study

A learning support assistant was asked to help Year 2 students who were not able to count forwards and backwards to 20 fluently. Her comments led to my carrying out a short piece of research involving 40 Year 2 students, 40 Year 6 students and 20 Key Stage 3 students. For the Year 2 and 6 age groups, half of the students were judged to have no difficulty with number and the other half were showing some cause for concern. 10 of the Key Stage 3 students were diagnosed as dyslexic and the others, in the same school, were not. All of the students were asked to count 1 to 20 forwards and backwards. They were then asked to sequence the numbers 1-20 written on cards. None of the students experienced difficulty in sequencing the numbers using a visual peg although observation noted that, particularly when sequencing the numbers backwards, 44 per cent of the students who were assessed as having difficulty with number laid the multiples of 2 and 'filled in the gaps'. Without the aid of the cards, 21 per cent of the total sample could not accurately count backwards. This figure rose to 54 per cent of those identified with difficulties and 100 per cent of the Key Stage 3 dyslexic students. Most of the students found difficulty with the numbers 13, 17 and 11. Counting forwards gave a success rate of 88 per cent but again, the 'stumbling blocks' were 13 and 17. All of the classrooms had multiplication squares on display but not 100 squares. The students could accurately give the sequence 2, 4, 6 . . . as the two-times table on display acted as constant reinforcement but could not place the prime numbers. Pollock and Waller (1999) state that counting backwards is difficult and that dyslexic students find this a particularly difficult exercise. The students who experienced difficulty with this exercise were given 100 squares in addition to multiplication squares to help with reinforcement of the relationship between numbers.

This study highlighted the need for visual representation of maths concepts at the very basic stages and that this may need to continue throughout the dyslexic student's maths career. The increased success rate when using the cards also highlights how multisensory material allowed the students to experiment with number, which they were unable to do as a purely abstract task.

Strategies

- The student can construct a 100 square. This can also be used to investigate other number patterns and relationships between numbers.
- Look at strategies for multiplication as discussed earlier in 'memory'.
- Use fraction pies or equivalent charts for fractions to act as visual representation of fractions. See Figure 15.

Figure 15 Chart to make equivalent fractions

- Encourage the student to rewrite calculations in a format that they can work with:

  24 + 37 becomes:
  24
  <u>37</u> +

- Promote understanding of the basic operations. It is also important to check that this understanding has taken place.
- Place value charts (Figure 16) can be an excellent tool to help with understanding of place value. When dividing and multiplying by 10, the student can write the original number and 'move' it using arrows and counting the number of places moved. Place value charts are an invaluable visual aid. They can be used to help with addition and subtraction and can be enlarged to accommodate Dienes equipment to help demonstrate concepts. Some students have difficulty with place value at GCSE level and can be encouraged to draw quickly a place value table as part of their 'working out' during exams if this helps with calculation or checking.

Thousand 1000	Hundred 100	Ten 10	Units 1	•Tenths $\frac{1}{10}$	Hundredths $\frac{1}{100}$	Thousandths $\frac{1}{1000}$

Figure 16 Place value chart

If a student experiences problems with place value during multiplication, the 'Chinese Box' (or 'Lattice') method may help (See Figure 17).

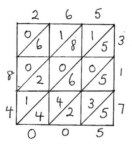

$$265 \times 317 = 84,005$$

Figure 17 Chinese box method

- Number lines, with positive and negative numbers clearly identified, can be constructed by the student. Again, students can construct a number line during examinations. However, the orientation of number lines can be crucial for some dyslexic students. A Year 9 student was having difficulty with a horizontal number line. She saw a pile of (identical) blank number lines and asked to use the one that happened to be facing her so that the line appeared to be vertical. She could use the line in this way as she could envisage it as a thermometer with the numbers getting larger as they 'went up'.
- When a student is required to order numbers, he may often find it easier to write the numbers vertically:

  6.067, 6.706, 0.67, 0.076, 0.607 would be written thus:

  6.067

  6.706

  0.670

  0.076

  0.607.

- The student can work systematically through this column and cross off each number as it is ordered. A system of reordering and crossing out numbers that have been calculated can be transferred to other topics. Students have found this useful in algebra.

  2a + 4b + 3a + 3c - 3b + 6c becomes:

  2a + 3a + 4b - 3b + 3c + 6c.

- While reordering numbers, the fact that the numbers have an operation attached is also reinforced as the student must remember to move the sign as well as the number. However, this strategy may not be effective for students who may miscopy numbers.

Orientation and shape

Difficulties with orientation can manifest when working with shape. The student may find that he cannot carry out transformations and finds geometry and trigonometry difficult.

Strategies

- Students can use tracing paper to trace and cut out the figure. This can be used to physically move the figure during transformations.
- Books and examination papers are movable objects. Encourage students to rotate books and papers.
- Some examination questions involve a combination of shapes which can be visually confusing. Students can cover parts of the shape that are not relevant to the immediate task in hand.

Case study

> Bobby's teacher could not understand why he was having sporadic success with questions on the Pythagoras theory. His participation during introduction of the topic indicated that he appeared to have grasped the concept, yet, when working through his textbook, this did not seem to be secure. Analysis of his errors soon highlighted that correct answers were given when the right angle appeared at the bottom left of the figure aligned with the edges of the book. This was how the teacher had introduced the figure and Bobby could not 'find' the right angle and work out the hypotenuse when the triangles had been rotated in the text book. Bobby was told to turn the textbook around until he could interpret the figure.

Sequencing and language

A student hearing or reading: 'Forty-five take away six' will write 45 - 6. However, when this is worded 'take six from forty-five' he may write 6 - 45. Similar problems are encountered with division. The student can also make errors of this sort or transpose figures when using a calculator.

Strategies

- When a student is observed making errors of this kind, discuss the wording in relationship to the calculation, and check whether the sum he has written 'looks right' (for example 6 - 45 would be unlikely).
- Encourage the student to adopt this method of checking independently.

Time

Telling the time, reading timetables and elapsed time may all be difficult for the dyslexic student.

Strategies

- A whole-class exercise, for the younger students, could be to construct a table of equivalents in hourly intervals, showing analogue time, digital time and words for both 12 and 24-hour systems.
- Students who still find difficulty in mastering this could make an individual table. It would be helpful if, when the student changes class at the end of the year, this could progress with him until this concept is secure. For some students, this may never happen and such tables will be needed throughout their statutory education career.

Motor skills

Difficulties

- The student may not be able to construct charts and diagrams accurately, measure and draw angles and geometrical figures, and carry out practical measuring tasks.
- The student may have difficulty in using such equipment as rulers, protractors and compasses.
- Written work may be poorly presented.
- Numbers and symbols may be written or copied inaccurately.
- Students may misalign numbers when copying or during calculation.

Strategies

- The Dyslexia Shop stocks fingertip rulers for older students, fun rulers for younger students and pencil grips for all age groups.
- Provide the student with sheets with pre-drawn axes for bar charts.
- Use a buddy system for measuring tasks. The student with poor motor skills can read the measurement while his partner carries out the practical element of the task.
- If the student's motor skills are very poor, it may be necessary to carry out measurement and drawing

for him. Ensure that the student participates fully and knows that the person acting as his hands is there simply for that function – the student will provide the ideas and information and describe how he wishes the final chart or drawing to look.

- Poor presentation should be treated sympathetically.
- Use squared paper to minimize misalignment of numbers and to help with accurate writing of numbers and symbols. Encourage the student to check the accuracy of work that he has copied.

Calculators

There are many opinions on the merits of the use of calculators but I feel that, generally, the use of a calculator can allow the dyslexic student greater freedom to explore mathematics. The higher 'success' rate in correct answers during calculation will also raise self-esteem which can lead to an increased confidence in tackling more complex concepts or calculations.

Advantages of the use of calculators

- Allows students to reach solutions.
- Promotes mathematical discussion.
- Requires the early development of estimating and approximating skills.
- Eases the transfer from concrete to symbolic thinking.
- Allows real-life numbers to be used.
- Allows mathematical exploration.
- Helps to focus on the problem rather than computation.
- Allows concentration on methods and concepts.
- Takes away some of the 'fear' of mathematics.

Disadvantages of using a calculator

- A student can get an answer but forget what has been done to achieve this.
- Different types of calculator and too many functions can cause confusion.
- Transposition of number from page to calculator can occur.
- Student may say 'multiply' but press 'add' button.
- Decimal points may be ignored (usually shown at the bottom of the display panel), or miskeyed in the wrong place.
- Commas, used to divide thousands, may be read as decimal points.
- Answers may be 'taken for granted' and not checked, especially by those with weak estimation skills.

7 The wider school community

Good communication with, and support from, all members of the school community who are involved in the learning experience and emotional well-being of the student are crucial to ensure a successful learning experience.

Working with parents

Many parents will be reluctant to approach the school with concerns regarding their child for fear of gaining a 'fussy parent' label, particularly during secondary education. This can raise anxiety levels which will, in turn, be conveyed to the student, regardless of how hard the parents try to hide their feelings.

The formal assessment process will be an emotional time for parents and student and may need to be handled sensitively. Parents may feel relieved that a diagnosis corroborates their concerns. Another may not wish for their child to be labelled, especially if the student is showing signs of low self-esteem or is being teased by his peers. The parents and child should be encouraged to view the assessment as a positive step forward in the student's learning experience.

The outcomes and recommendations of the report should be discussed with the parents and student. Even the younger student should be encouraged to take some ownership of his learning; recognition of his strengths and weaknesses will help him to develop the skills that he will need later for independent learning. My experience in coordinating support for students in a college of further education has indicated that the students who have a sound understanding of how dyslexia affects their learning have been able to enter into productive discussion of their needs and have quickly, confidently and successfully used the support offered. Parents will have the opportunity to question the past and potential impact on their child's learning and can gain a clearer view of their roles in his future learning. Parents who have tried, seemingly unsuccessfully, to help their child in the past may feel insecure in their ability to help the student in the future. Giving parents a clearly defined role in an intervention programme should help to support their child's learning in the home and at school.

> Productive communication between home and school is paramount in supporting the emotional well-being of parents and students alike, and in helping students achieve a successful shared outcome to their learning.

How parents can help

- Enlist the support of parents to play a part in the implementation of a programme of intervention. This is particularly useful for the reinforcement and practice of new skills.
- Parents may purchase books on dyslexia or obtain information via the internet. This has the potential to cause confusion as intervention programmes or strategies for study suggested in a book may not match those that are thought to be most effective for a particular student. Discussion with the parents may be necessary for reassurance. Nevertheless, it may transpire that the parents have successfully tried a suggestion from a book at home and it may be possible to integrate this into the classroom. Discussion regarding methods of study at home will make the parents feel that they are able to play a significant part in their child's learning and they may also be able to impart useful information for the teacher to use.
- Encourage the parents to take and exhibit a positive view of the student's dyslexia. It is an uphill task for the teacher to help the student to maintain his self-esteem if this is being eroded in the home. It is also confusing for the student to receive mixed messages about his strengths, weaknesses and like-lihood of future success.
- Maintain good lines of communication regarding the student's progress. The parents will be far happier to let the teacher direct the support given in the home if they have a clear picture of both current achievement and future goals.
- Give parents details of topics currently being studied. Parents and student may then be able to research and discuss the topic. In certain subject areas it may be possible to make this a multisensory experience by visiting a museum, role-playing a literary or historical event, watching a DVD or simply making a collage or drawing around the topic. There are many maths games and puzzles available that parents can use at home. This will reinforce information and gives the student the potential to exhibit knowledge of the subject in school either by explanation or demonstration of work carried out at home. The student can also develop research and recording skills in media other than the written word.
- Ensure that parents understand that, even with intervention, progress will be slower for the dyslexic student than his peers or other children in the family. Parents have expressed concerns that inter-vention 'is not working' when the student does not appear to have 'caught up'.
- Ask parents to inform you of any recent successes in areas of the student's life outside of school. The student who is suffering low self-esteem may not have a positive view of any achievements. The teacher can help to reinforce praise given by parents.
- It may help if parents are given precise details of study plans. Many believe that the dyslexic student has to study or revise for longer or more intensively than his peers. Use the chapter on memory in this book

to explain the rationale behind the 'little and often' rule. For the older student, it may help if the teacher and student devise revision timetables which parents can supervise.

- Home-school diaries are an excellent idea for dyslexic students of all ages. Parents are usually required to sign the student's homework diaries every week but this is not an appropriate medium through which to express concerns as the diaries may be viewed in the classroom and can be seen by other students. A separate notebook could be used on a two-way basis to record progress and concerns as they arise. This may not need to be a weekly or daily 'report' which may place an unnecessary burden on busy parents and teachers.
- Ask parents to check homework diaries to ensure that homework is handed in on time, correct equipment is brought to school and that homework is understood correctly.
- Parents can help at home with paired reading for students of any age.
- Parents may be willing to record text for students if this is deemed to be the most effective way of study.
- Parents can help support maths learning by involving students in everyday tasks such as counting change and estimating totals when shopping, weighing and measuring, map reading and estimating distance.

Working with support staff

Often, especially in secondary school, the learning support assistant (LSA) will have the most frequent and closest contact with the dyslexic student. The LSA may be working with several students across the whole curriculum which can make communication with all staff a time-consuming and logistically difficult issue. However, the use of support staff can be most effective when the following strategies are put in place.

- Dyslexia training should be available for all support staff. This can take the form of an accredited course or single day Continuing Professional Development or INSET courses. Dyslexia Action will be able to advise the school on suitable accredited courses.
- The LSA should have access to or be given relevant information from the dyslexic student's assessment report to enable her to have a clear insight into the needs of the individual student.
- The LSA should be actively involved in the continuing assessment of the student's progress and needs. There should be a mechanism for her to record any information that she believes is relevant to the student's learning experience.
- It can be extremely valuable if the LSA can meet with the specialist teacher, SENCO and, where possible, parents to ensure that her role in any intervention programme is as effective as it can be.
- The LSA should be allowed an input during reviews of support given to the student. For example, if the older student has developed a strong 'buddy' system with a peer in one subject area, the LSA may feel that this is a far more effective way of him developing independent learning skills and may wish to 'take a back seat' more often in that particular class.

Using support staff effectively

The role of the learning support assistant will vary for many reasons including the needs of the students, ethos of the school and number of support staff within the school. Most schools make excellent and innovative use of support staff, some of which have been mentioned in earlier chapters in this book, but it would not be possible to list all of the ways that support staff can be used effectively. However, the following strategies would seem to be desirable where resources permit.

- One-on-one or small group help for reading, spelling and writing. This may be an effective way of using support staff to reinforce the work carried out by the student with a specialist teacher. Many schools use programmes designed for use by the non-specialist teacher and these are delivered by support staff.
- One-on-one or small group support for the older student to help develop effective study skills.
- In-class support. At Key Stages 3 and 4, in-class support is often not welcomed by the student, particularly when the learning support assistant sits next to the student for the whole lesson. The situation is often more comfortable for the student when the LSA 'floats' around the rest of the class, giving help to the dyslexic student when it is needed (for example, if text needs to be read or notes taken).
- Differentiation. As mentioned in Chapter 3, differentiation is not simply writing worksheets in more simple language. Effective differentiation takes into account the student's strengths, weaknesses, learning styles and motivational factors. Very often, the LSA who works closely with the student will be best positioned to have good knowledge of these. It is beneficial to the student if the class teacher discusses differentiation with the LSA. Depending on skills and qualifications, some LSAs are keen to differentiate work for the student according to the ethos of the school.
- Instigate a clear means of communication with the LSA. This could be by internal communication, regular one-on-one meetings and including LSAs in departmental meetings (one school has a ten-minute SEN slot at the start of departmental meetings at which support staff are welcome).
- Involve the LSA in the student's monitoring process. If necessary, give specific areas with regards to progress, ongoing difficulty or behaviours for her to observe and record.
- Many students view the LSA as 'less frightening' than the teacher and may divulge fears, feelings of low self-esteem and other concerns. Occasionally, this can be quite upsetting for the LSA and she may need the support of another member of staff. There should also be a mechanism for her to record any concerns regarding the student's emotional well-being.
- The LSA should be consulted when Individual Education Plans or Individual Learning Plans are being reviewed.

> **The Learning Support Assistant often has the greatest amount of individual contact with the student and must be viewed as an important member of the team involved in the student's learning and emotional well-being.**

Suggested further reading:

How to Survive and Succeed as a Teaching Assistant by Veronica Birkett.

Help Students Improve Their Study Skills: A Handbook for Teaching Assistants in Secondary Schools by Jane Dupree.

Encouraging positive peer attitude

The student who lacks confidence in his abilities and has low self-esteem may often not feel 'part of the group' which will have a further detrimental effect on his self-esteem. He may feel that his peers take a negative view of his abilities which can lead to a reluctance to participate in group activities or to ask peers for help .He may not wish to display his strengths in case these are deemed inconsequential or mocked. The student who has difficulty with processing verbal language or with self-expression may feel that he does not 'fit in' socially.

These problems can seem insurmountable to the student who tries to tackle these alone. These social difficulties can act as a demotivating factor to learning.

Teachers, support staff and parents should all watch for signs of teasing or bullying. The school's bullying policy should be implemented as soon as possible if it is suspected that the student's peers are involved in such activity.

The use of group work can allow the student to display his strengths. It may be necessary to allot him specific tasks, geared to his strengths or involve him in discussion if he is reluctant to be an active group member. Any comments implying that the student is underachieving which could be picked up by other students in the class should be avoided.

'Buddy systems' are an effective way of encouraging good peer relationships. Failures in this system are often caused when one of the students feels that he is 'carrying' the other or doing the majority of the work. As this is likely to be the student who is not dyslexic this can have a disastrous effect on the dyslexic student's self-esteem. Buddy systems are most effective when each partner brings a strength to the partnership that supports the weakness in the other. For example, the dyslexic student may be able to understand quickly how to carry out an experiment in science and predict the outcome. He can demonstrate this to his partner who can record the findings; a task which the dyslexic student finds difficult. A case study of a successful pairing can be found in Chapter 2.

Dyslexic students often think differently and develop wonderfully innovative ways of tackling problems. Encourage the dyslexic student and, indeed, all students, to share their different ways of thinking and to value each other's thinking and learning styles. I have witnessed classes in which the dyslexic student's imaginative way of thinking has, over time, gained the admiration of his peers and his opinions and explanations become respected and valued.

Contacts, further reading and suppliers

Contacts

British Dyslexia Association
Tel: 0118 996 2677
www.bdadyslexia.org.uk

Dyslexia Action
Tel: 01784 222300
www.dyslexiaaction.org.uk

Dyspraxia Foundation
Tel: 01462 454 986
www.dypraxiafoundation.org.uk

NASEN (National Association for Special Educational Needs)
Tel: 01827 311500
www.nasen.org.uk

National Centre for Excellence in the Teaching of Maths (NCETM)
www.ncetm.org.uk

Quality Improvement Agency (QIA)
www.qia.org.uk

Further reading

Birkett, V. (2003), *How to Survive and Succeed as a Teaching Assistant* (Wisbech: LDA).

Buzan, T. and Buzan, B. (2000), *The Mind Map Book* (London: BBC Worldwide Ltd).

Buzan, T. (2003), *Mind Maps for Kids: An Introduction. The Shortcut to Success at School* (London: HarperCollins Publishers Ltd).

Buzan, T. (2005), *Mind Maps for Kids: Max Your Memory and Concentration* (London: HarperCollins Publishers Ltd).

Also see the Buzan website: www.mind-map.com.

Cogan, J. and Flecker, M. (2006), *Dyslexia in Secondary School* (London: Whurr).

Davis, M., Rankin, Q. and Riley, H. (2007), *Including Dyslexics: Indicators of Dyslexia in Art Students*. Drawings available at www.designage.rca.ac.uk/kt/include/2007/proceedings/paper.

Davis, R. (1997), *The Gift of Dyslexia: Why Some of the Brightest People Can't Read and How They Can Learn* (2nd revised edition) (London: Souvenir Press Ltd).

Dupree, J. (2005), *Help Students Improve Their Study Skills: A Handbook for Teaching Assistants in Secondary Schools* (London: David Fulton Publishers).

Hornsby, B. (1995), *Overcoming Dyslexia* (London: Random House Ltd).

Hornsby, B., Shear, F. and Pool, J. (1999), *Alpha to Omega: The A-Z of Teaching Reading, Writing and Spelling* (Oxford: Heinemann Educational Publishers).

Miles, T. and Westcome, J. (2001), *Music and Dyslexia: Opening New Doors* (London: Whurr).

Moody, S. (2004), *Dyslexia: A Teenager's Guide* (London: Random House UK Ltd).

Mortimer, T. (2006), *Dyslexia and Learning Style: A Practitioner's Handbook* (London: Whurr).

Moseley, D. (1991), *ACE Spelling Dictionary* (LDA).

Ott, P. (1997), *How to Detect and Manage Dyslexia: A Reference and Resource Manual* (Oxford: Heinemann Educational Publishers).

Pollock, J. and Waller, E. (1999), *Day-To-Day Dyslexia in the Classroom* (London: Routledge).

Raymond, S. (2001), *Supporting Dyslexic Pupils 7-14 Across the Curriculum* (London: David Fulton Publishers).

Reid, G. (2007), *Dyslexia* (2nd edition) (London: Continuum International Publishing Group).

Sassoon, R. (2003), *Handwriting: The Way To Teach It* (2nd edition) (London: Paul Chapman Educational Publishing).

Sassoon, R. (2006), *Handwriting Problems in the Secondary School* (London: Paul Chapman Educational Publishing).

Snowling, M. and Stackhouse, J. (2005), *Dyslexia, Speech and Language: A Practitioner's Handbook* (2nd revised edition) (London: Whurr).

Further reading – Maths

Butterworth, B. and Yeo, D. (2004), *Dyscalculia Guidance: Helping Pupils with Specific Learning Difficulties in Maths* (London: NFER Nelson Publishing Co. Ltd).

Chinn, S. (1997), *What to Do When You Can't Learn the Times Tables* (Baldock: Egon Publishers Ltd).

Chinn, S. (1999), *What to Do When You Can't Add and Subtract* (Baldock: Egon Publishers Ltd).

Chinn, S. (2004), *The Trouble With Maths* (London: Routledge Farmer).

Chinn, S. (2007), *Dealing With Dyscalculia. Sum Hope^2* (London: Souvenir Press Ltd).

Chinn, S. J. and Ashcroft, J. R. (1998), *Mathematics for Dyslexics: A Teaching Handbook* (2nd edition) (London: Whurr).

Clayton, P. (2003), *How to Develop Numeracy in Children with Dyslexia* (Cambridge: LDA).

Henderson, A. (1998), *Maths for the Dyslexic: A Practical Guide* (London: David Fulton Publishers).

Henderson, A., Came, F. and Brough, M. (2003), *Working with Dyscalculia* (Marlborough: Learning Works International Ltd).

Kay, J. and Yeo, D. (2005), *Dyslexia and Maths* (London: David Fulton Publishers Ltd).

Miles, T. R. and Miles, E. (2004), *Dyslexia and Mathematics* (2nd edition) (London: Routledge Falmer).

Quality Improvement Agency (2007), *Improving Learning in Mathematics*, available at http://teachingandlearning.qia.org.uk.

Robson, P. (2006), *Maths Dictionary* (Scarborough: Newby Books).

Yeo, D. (2003), *Dyslexia, Dyspraxia and Mathematics* (London: Whurr).

Suppliers

Anne Arbor Publishers Limited
Tel: 01668 214460
www.annarbor.co.uk

Barrington Stoke
Tel: 0131 225 4113
www.barringtonstoke.co.uk

Cerium Visual Technologies.
Tel: 01580 765 211
www.ceriumvistech.co.uk

Crossbow Education
Tel: 01785 660 902
www.crossboweducation.com

Dyslexia Action
Tel: 01784 222300
www.dyslexiaaction.org.uk

Harcourt Assessment
Tel: 01865 888188
www.harcourt-uk.com

Iansyst
Tel: 01223 420101 (product advice)
www.dyslexic.com

LDA
Tel: 0845 120 4776
www.ldalearning.com

New Leaf Publications
Tel: 07984 241 863
www.newleafbooks.org.uk

nferNelson Shop
Tel: 0845 602 1937
www.shop.nfer-nelson.co.uk

Partners in Education UK Ltd
Tel: 01707 642745
www.partnersineducation.co.uk

The Dyslexia Shop
Tel: 0131 672 1552
www.thedyslexiashop.co.uk

THRASS (Teaching Handwriting Reading and Spelling Skills)
www.thrass.co.uk

Bibliography

Baddeley, A. and Hitch, G. (1974), 'Working Memory' in Bower, G. A. (ed), *The Psychology of Learning and Motivation: Advances in Research and Theory*, Vol. 8, pp. 48–79 (New York: Academic Press).

Birkett, V. (2003), *How to Survive and Succeed as a Teaching Assistant* (Wisbech: LDA).

Bowers, P. G. and Wolfe, M. (1993), 'Theoretical links between naming speed, precise timing mechanism and orthographic skills in dyslexia'. *Reading and Writing: An Interdisciplinary Journal*, 5, 69–85.

British Dyslexia Association (2006), *The Dyslexia Handbook 2006* (Reading: The British Dyslexia Association).

British Dyslexia Association (2007). Available at www.bdadyslexia.org.uk.

Butterworth, B. (2003), *Dyscalculia Screener* (London: NFER Nelson Publishing Group).

Butterworth, B. and Yeo, D. (2004), *Dyscalculia Guidance: Helping Pupils with Specific Learning Difficulties in Maths* (London: NFER Nelson Publishing Co. Ltd).

Buzan, T. (2000), *Use Your Head* (London: BBC Worldwide Ltd).

Buzan, T. (2003), *Mind Maps for Kids: An Introduction. The Shortcut to Success at School* (London: HarperCollins Publishers Ltd).

Buzan, T. (2005), *Mind Maps for Kids: Max Your Memory and Concentration* (London: HarperCollins Publishers Ltd).

Buzan, T. and Buzan, B. (2000), *The Mind Map Book* (London: BBC Worldwide Limited).

Chinn, S. (1997), *What to Do When You Can't Learn the Times Tables* (Baldock: Egon Publishers Ltd).

Chinn, S. (1999), *What to Do When You Can't Add and Subtract* (Baldock: Egon Publishers Ltd).

Chinn, S. (2004), *The Trouble With Maths* (London: Routledge Falmer).

Chinn, S. (2007), *Dealing With Dyscalculia: Sum Hope²* (London: Souvenir Press Ltd).

Chinn, S. J. and Ashcroft, J. R. (1998), *Mathematics for Dyslexics: A Teaching Handbook* (2nd edition) (London: Whurr).

Cowling, H. and Cowling, K. (1993), *Toe By Toe* (Shipley: Keda Publishing).

Craik and Lockhart (1972) in Anderson, J. R. (1995), *Cognitive Psychologies and its Implication* (4th edition) (New York: W. H. Freeman and Co.).

Davis, M., Rankin, Q. and Riley, H. (2007), *Including Dyslexics: Indicators of Dyslexia in Art Students' Drawings*. Available at www.designage.rca.ac.uk/kt/include/2007/proceedings/paper.

Davis, R. (1997), *The Gift of Dyslexia: Why Some of the Brightest People Can't Read and How They Can Learn* (2nd revised edition) (London: Souvenir Press Ltd).

Department for Education and Skills (2007), *The National Numeracy Strategy: Guidance to Support Pupils with Dyslexia and Dyscalculia*. Available from www.dfs.gov.uk.

Dienes, Z. P. (1960), 'Building up Mathematics' in Miles, T. R. and Miles, E. (1992), *Dyslexia and Mathematics* (London: Routledge).

Dupree, J. (2005), *Help Students Improve Their Study Skills. A Handbook for Teaching Assistants in Secondary Schools* (London: David Fulton Publishers).

Dyslexia Action. Available at www.dyslexiaaction.org.uk.

Ebbinghaus, H. (1913), *Memory: A Contribution to Experimental Psychology* (New York: Teacher's College Columbia University).

Fawcett, A. and Nicolson, R. (2004), *Dyslexia Early Screening Test Second Edition (DEST-2)* (Oxford: Harcourt Assessment).

Fawcett, A. and Nicolson, R. (2004), *Dyslexia Screening Test – Junior (DST-J)* (Oxford: Harcourt Assessment).

Fawcett, A. and Nicolson, R. (2004), *Dyslexia Screening Test – Secondary (DST-S)* (Oxford: Harcourt Assessment).

Fellgett, P. (1986), 'Living with Dyslexia', in Ott, P. (1997), *How to Detect and Manage Dyslexia. A Reference and Resource Manual* (Oxford: Heinemann Educational Publishers).

Frith, U. (1995), 'Beneath the surface of developmental dyslexia', in K. E. Patterson, J. C. Marshall and M. Coltheart (eds), *Surface Dyslexia* (London: Erlbaum).

Frith, U., Pidgeon, E. and Ramus, F. (2002), 'The relationship between motor control and phonology in dyslexic children'. *Journal of Child Psychology and Psychiatry and Allied Disciplines*, 44 (5), 712–22.

Galaburda, A. M. et al. (1985), *Ann. Neurol.*, 29, 315–19.

Galaburda, A. M. et al. (1987), 'Planum temporale asymmetry: Repraisal since Geschwind and Levitsky', *Neuropsychologia*, 25 (6), 853–68, in Miles, T. R. and Miles, E. (1999), *Dyslexia – A Hundred Years On* (Bristol: J. W. Arrowsmith).

Geschwind, N. and Levitsky, W. (1968), 'Human brain; left-right asymmetries in temporal speech region'. *Science*, 161, 186–7, in Miles, T. R. and Miles, E. (1999), *Dyslexia – A Hundred Years On* (Bristol: J. W. Arrowsmith).

Gillingham, A. and Stillman, B. W. (1960), *Remedial Training for Children with Specific Disability in Reading, Spelling and Penmanship* (7th edition) (Cambridge, MA: Educators Publishing Service).

Grant, D. (2004), *Dyslexia When Combined with Chronic Medical Conditions.* Available at www.nadp-uk.org.

Henderson, A. (1998), *Maths for the Dyslexic: A Practical Guide* (London: David Fulton Publishers).

Henderson, A., Came, F. and Brough, M. (2003), *Working with Dyscalculia* (Marlborough: Learning Works International Ltd).

Herstein, I. N. (1975), *Topics in Algebra* (Chichester: Wiley).

Hornsby, B., Shear, F. and Pool, J. (2006), *Alpha to Omega Teacher's Handbook. The A-Z of Teaching Reading, Writing and Spelling* (6th edition revised and updated by Dyslexia Action) (Oxford: Heinemann Educational Publishers).

Hulme, C. and Joshi, R. M. (1998), *Reading and Spelling: Development and Disorder* (Hillsdale, NJ: Lawrence Erlbaum Associates Inc. US).

Irlen (2007). Available at www.irlen.com.

Izard, J. F., Miller, K. M. and Vernon, P. E. (2005), *Mathematics Competency Test* (London: Hodder and Stoughton).

Klare, G. R. (1963), *The Measure of Readability* (Iowa: Iowa State University Press).

Liebeck, P. (1984), *How Children Learn Mathematics – A Guide for Parents and Teachers* (Middlesex: Penguin Books Ltd).

Miles, E. (1997), *The Bangor Dyslexia Teaching System* (3rd revised edition) (London: Whurr).

Miles, T. R. and Miles, E. (1992), *Dyslexia and Mathematics* (London: Routledge).

Miles, T. R. and Miles, E. (2004), *Dyslexia and Mathematics* (2nd edition) (London: Routledge Falmer).

Miles, T. and Westcome, J. (2001) *Music and Dyslexia: Opening New Doors* (London, Whurr).

Miller, G. A. (1956), 'The magical number seven plus or minus two: Some limitations on our capacity for processing information'. *Psychological Review*, 63(2), 81–96.

Moody, S. (2004), *Dyslexia: A Teenager's Guide* (London: Random House UK Ltd).

Murdock, B. B. (1962), 'The serial positional effect of free recall'. *Journal of Experimental Psychology*, 64, 482–8.

National Literacy Strategy (2001), *Developing Early Writing* (Nottingham: DfES Publications).

Newman, R. M. (1998), *Developmental Perspectives on Dyscalculia: Implications for*

Teaching in the Middle and Secondary School. Available at http://www.dyscalculia.org/Edu562.html p.19.

Ott, P. (1997), *How to Detect and Manage Dyslexia. A Reference and Resource Manual* (Oxford: Heinemann Educational Publishers).

Palmenti, J. (2000) *Success is Never Boring*. Available at www.dyslexia-gibraltar.com.

Paulascu, Frith, Snowling et al. (1996), in Samuelson, E. (coll), 'Dyslexia Update: Recent Research and Development'.

Pollock, J. and Waller, E. (1999), *Day-To-Day Dyslexia in the Classroom* (London: Routledge).

Rashoote, C. A., Torgesen, J. K. and Wagner, R. K. (1999), *Comprehensive Test of Phonological Processing; Examiner's Manual* (Austin, Texas: PRO-ED Inc.).

Raymond, S. (2001), *Supporting Dyslexic Pupils 7–14 Across the Curriculum* (London: David Fulton Publishers).

Reid, G. (2007), *Dyslexia* (2nd edition) (London: Continuum International Publishing Group).

Robson, P. (2006), *Maths Dictionary* (Scarborough: Newby Books).

Sahlberg, P. and Berry, J. (2002), 'One and one is sometimes three in small group mathematics learning'. *Asia Pacific Journal of Education*, 22 (1), 83–94. Available at www.tech.plym.ac.uk.

Sassoon, R. (2003), *Handwriting: The Way To Teach It* (2nd edition) (London: Paul Chapman Educational Publishing).

Sassoon, R. (2006), *Handwriting Problems in the Secondary School* (London: Paul Chapman Educational Publishing).

Snowling, M. and Stackhouse, J. (2005) *Dyslexia, Speech and Language: A Practitioner's Handbook* (2nd revised edition) (London: Whurr).

Stein, J. F. and Walsh, V. (1997), 'To see but not to read: The magnocellular theory of dyslexia'. *Trends Neurosci.*, 20, 147–52.

Swann, M. (2007), *Towards More Active Learning Approaches*. Available in www.maths4life.org.

Tallal, P. (1984), 'Temporal or phonetic processing difficulties in dyslexia? That is the question'. *Applied Psycholinguistics*, 5, 167–9.

Tallal, P., Miller, S., Jenkins, B. and Merzenich, M. (1997), 'The role of temporal processing in developmental language-based learning disorders: Research and clinical implications', in Blachman, B. (ed.), *Foundations of Reading Acquisition* (Mahwah, NJ: Erlbaum), pp. 49–66.

Vellutino, F. R. and Scanlon, D. M. (1991), 'The pre-eminence of phonologically based skills in learning to read', in Brady, S. and Shanweiler, D. (eds), *Phonological Processes in Literacy; A Tribute to Isabelle Liberman* (Hillsdale, NJ: Lawrence Erlbaum Associates Inc. US), pp 237–57.

Yeo, D. (2003), *Dyslexia, Dyspraxia and Mathematics* (London: Whurr).

Index